SECOND EDITION

HOW TO SAY THE
RIGHT
THING
EVERY TIME

To Dawn McDowell, who taught me a lot about how to say the right thing every time.

SECOND EDITION

HOW TO SAY THE
RIGHT
THING
EVERY TIME

**Communicating Well
With Students, Staff,
Parents, and the Public**

ROBERT D. RAMSEY

CORWIN
PRESS
A SAGE Company

For information:

Corwin Press, Inc.
A SAGE Company
2455 Teller Road
Thousand Oaks, California 91320
E-mail: order@corwinpress.com

SAGE Ltd.
6 Bonhill Street
London EC2A 4PU
United Kingdom

SAGE India Pvt. Ltd.
M-32 Market
Greater Kailash I
New Delhi 110 048 India

SAGE Asia-Pacific Pte. Ltd.
33 Pekin Street #02-01
Far East Square
Singapore 048763

Printed in the United States of America

Library of Congress Cataloging-in-Publication Data

Ramsey, Robert D.
  How to say the right thing every time : communicating well with students, staff, parents and the public / Robert D. Ramsey.—2nd ed.
      p. cm.
Includes bibliographical references and index.
ISBN 978-1-4129-6407-4 (cloth)
ISBN 978-1-4129-6408-1 (pbk.)
  1. Communication in education—Handbooks, manuals, etc. 2. Oral communication—Handbooks, manuals, etc. 3. Interaction analysis in education—Handbooks, manuals, etc. 4. School administrators—Handbooks, manuals, etc. I. Title.

LB1033.5.R36 2009
371.102'2—dc22   2008004874

This book is printed on acid-free paper.

08   09   10   11   10 9 8 7 6 5 4 3 2 1

Acquisitions Editor:	Arnis Burvikovs
Associate Editor:	Megan Bedell
Production Editor:	Appingo Publishing Services
Cover Designer:	Scott Van Atta

Contents

List of Boxes

Preface

Managers today must be effective communicators. . . .
Without effective communication, the vision is lost.
                                          —Patricia M. Buhler

How to Say the Right Thing Every Time is a breakthrough guide, tailor-made to help school leaders know what to say and how to say it in every situation when dealing with students, parents, colleagues, the general public, and the media. It represents a next-generation communication tool and breaks new ground by equipping practitioners in the field with tips, tools, rules, and pointers needed to communicate successfully in all situations.

This is the first-ever sourcebook overflowing with insider information about what works and what doesn't in communicating with each of the school's diverse publics and constituencies. Better yet, it pinpoints all the basic components to allow readers to create their own customized messages, using their own words in their own way.

Each chapter is packed with school-tested guidelines, specific do's and don'ts, suggested power words, and real-world examples to help all educators reach their audience by knowing exactly what to say (or write) and how to say it.

There is no other guide on the market today that is designed to help *all* school leaders put *all* their spoken and written messages across to *all* of the school's multiple audiences.

Highlights of the text include such hard-hitting topics as:

- The Twenty Biggest Communication Mistakes School Leaders Make and How to Avoid Them
- Dealing With Touchy Topics (Alcohol, Drugs, Sex . . .)
- The Proper Art of Bitching
- How to Talk to Tough Kids (Including Gang Members)
- What to Say to Angry, Out-of-Control Parents
- How to Talk to Kids About National Tragedies (New)
- And Much More

WHAT'S NEW IN THE SECOND EDITION?

In response to reader requests, this new edition has been updated throughout, popular features have been expanded, and important new material has been added—including a powerful new chapter on "How to Target Communication to All Stakeholders."

If you are like most school leaders, you spend much of your time informing, instructing, inspiring, explaining, advising, questioning, convincing, persuading, coaching, coaxing, and cajoling many audiences in a variety of settings. These functions are too important to be left to chance. Now, you don't have to.

How to Say the Right Thing Every Time takes the concept of "communication guide" to a new level and offers better career-saving communication advice than any other resource available today. Period!

If you want to be a better communicator and a better school leader, this guide may be just what you've been looking for. You will never know unless you look. There's no extra charge for starting now.

Acknowledgments

Writing is a process of becoming indebted. In creating this particular book, I am most indebted to Connie Kallback, who helped spawn the idea and nurture it during the embryonic state; Robb Clouse, whose editorial vision brought it to fruition; Lisa Allen, whose copyediting expertise polished the second edition; and Joyce Ramsey, whose word-processing wizardry produced a viable manuscript.

—R.D.R.

Publisher's Acknowledgments

Corwin Press gratefully acknowledges the contributions of the following reviewers:

Russ Bennett, Superintendent
Aurora City Schools, Aurora, OH

Marie Blum, Superintendent
Canaseraga Central School District, Canaseraga, NY

Anne Giddings, Assistant Superintendent
Ansonia Public Schools, Cheshire, CT

James Kelleher, Assistant Superintendent
Scituate Public Schools, Scituate, MA

Joyce Uglow, Principal
Dyer Intermediate School, Burlington, WI

About the Author

 **Robert D. Ramsey** (EdD) is a lifelong educator and freelance writer. His extensive career at three award-winning school districts in two different states includes frontline experience as a teacher, counselor, supervisor, curriculum coordinator, human resources director, associate superintendent, acting superintendent, and adjunct professor. Currently, he and his wife, Joyce, live in Minneapolis where they can be close to their two grown children and four grandchildren.

Dr. Ramsey is the author of twenty successful professional books and a frequent contributor to numerous popular journals and newspapers. His most recent publications include *What Matters Most to School Leaders* (2005); *Lead, Follow, or Get Out of the Way*, 2nd edition (2006); and *Don't Teach the Canaries Not to Sing* (2008).

Throughout his distinguished career, Dr. Ramsey's communication skills have allowed him to help countless educators reach their full potential. Now in this revised edition of *How to Say the Right Thing Every Time*, he makes the latest and most effective strategies for communicating with students, parents, colleagues, the general public, and the media readily available to all school leaders.

The best advice is to say the right thing or say nothing.
—Harvey MacKay

The Twenty Biggest Communication Mistakes School Leaders Make and How to Avoid Them

Winning communication is the result of making small, insignificant adjustments in what you say and how you say it.

—Paul W. Swets

Words have power. They can be helpers, healers, revealers, and eye-openers—or they can be dangerous and hurtful weapons. That's why what people say and write to each other and how they say it is incredibly important. Educators know this better than anyone.

Education is communication. It's what school leaders do for a living. While the average person may speak and write up to 18,000 words each day, that's just a warm-up for most administrators and teachers, who are constantly communicating with the school's multiple and diverse audiences. If they do it right, their words inform, instruct, inspire, and, sometimes change lives forever.

When school leaders communicate effectively, students learn, parents and community members understand and support what the school is doing, and the process of teaching and learning moves forward. But when educators fail to communicate fully, misinformation, misinterpretations, misunderstandings, and mixed messages can cause the system's wheels to spin or come off altogether.

Unfortunately, even professionals don't always get it right. That's why it should come as no surprise that administrators and teachers sometimes have difficulty sending clear messages. Even the best school leaders don't always know the right thing to say or how to say it. Educators can have as much trouble communicating clearly as anyone else. Sometimes, more.

THE TOP TWENTY REASONS EDUCATORS FAIL TO COMMUNICATE

How many times have students in your school misunderstood directions or left class with no clear idea of the next day's assignment? How many kids are confused about exactly what behavior is expected, preferred, accepted, allowed, or valued in your school? If pressed, how many of your staff members would admit to being unclear about what the school's real priorities are? How many parents have left a parent-teacher conference in your school wondering if they had just received good news or bad news? Finally, how many times has a bond issue or referendum failed in your district because school officials didn't get their message across to taxpayers?

Unless you work in some kind of educational utopia, the correct response to all of the above is, "Too many!"

In a school environment, communication is the lifeblood of teaching and learning. Edu-leaders wear many hats, but first and foremost, they must be good communicators. Yet all educators fail to be understood sometimes. A few even make a habit of it. If you think it doesn't happen in your school, you're not paying attention.

It's not that school leaders intend to be obscure. Most try extremely hard to communicate about problems and solutions in clear-cut and meaningful ways. Yet many people (kids and adults alike) think that educators speak some goofy foreign language all their own ("educationese"). It's not uncommon for laymen to wonder just what educational leaders are really saying or talking about.

Mixed messages, confusing signals, and murky meanings don't have to happen in schools. But they do. Every day. Why is that?

As it turns out, there are twenty common mistakes that most often cause school leaders to communicate ineffectively. Superintendents make them. Principals and teachers do too. Fortunately, all are avoidable or correctable. After all, communication skills are learned, not God-given.

Here they are—the top twenty most serious communication mistakes educators make today (no priority ranking is intended or implied):

1. *Overreliance on jargon.* School leaders know a special language of technical, professional, and scientific (or pseudoscientific) terms. Unfortunately, kids, parents, and community members don't. When educators use too much insider talk they leave others out.

2. *Walking on eggs.* Educators love to soft-pedal issues and pussyfoot around touchy topics to avoid hurting anyone's feelings. It doesn't work. ("You can't make an omelet without breaking some eggs." —Anonymous)

3. *Bending over backward to be politically correct.* By taking extreme measures to avoid offending anyone's sensitivities, educators can end up saying too little, saying the wrong thing, or saying nothing and appearing ridiculous in the process. Neutered communication is often ineffectual communication.

4. *Too much formality.* When school leaders talk like a textbook, it turns others off and comes across as distant, aloof, and stuffy. It's OK for professionals to talk like real human beings and to use shirtsleeve language to get their points across.

5. *Overgeneralization.* Educators know better than anyone that all kids are different, that labels don't always fit, and that glittering generalities often confuse and mislead. Yet many persist in using them. Generalities don't work and people resent them. Specific facts and examples are still the best tools for breaking down communication barriers.

6. *Sermonizing.* There's a difference between teaching and preaching. When school leaders cross the line, communication always suffers. Kids, especially, tune out pontificating.

7. *Obfuscation.* Like politicians, educators are notorious for making things vague. It drives pupils and patrons nuts. When people want to pin you down, let them. That's when real communication takes place.

8. *Practicing dogmatism.* Being dogmatic is easy, but it doesn't facilitate communication. Nobody likes or listens to a "know-it-all," even when it's a superintendent, principal, or teacher. Effective school leaders help people discover information, answers, and solutions, instead of shoving material down their throats.

9. *Patronizing.* Talking down to students, staff members, parents, or community members is a surefire way to make them deaf to your message. Students, in particular, may not know what patronizing is, but they know they don't like it and they won't respond to it.

10. *Making empty threats.* An empty threat is a promise that can't be kept. Some educators aren't above using them

anyway. A prime example is when school administrators and board members "threaten" the public with unlikely larger class sizes if they don't vote for increased funding. Likewise, teachers sometimes threaten classes with unrealistic penalties. Such false threats are transparent. People recognize them for what they really are—lies. Threats that everyone knows can't be delivered destroy credibility. Real threats and real consequences get real results. Phony threats only cause people to disbelieve or to quit paying attention altogether. So much for communication.

11. *Whining.* Too many educators whine too much. It's a self-defeating communication strategy. School leaders may have a lot to complain about, but sniveling and seeking sympathy doesn't help. You can invite people to a "pity party," but most won't show up. Whining isn't communication. It's just an irritation.

12. *Grammatical and/or spelling errors.* When a superintendent, principal, or teacher sends out a memo or gives a speech full of errors, people pay attention. They talk about the mistakes; they remember them. And they forget what was really said. It happens more often than you think. Nothing kills credibility faster than simple mechanical mistakes. People notice. It makes a difference. When an audience is hung up on mistakes, it won't get the message.

13. *Lying and denying.* It's always a mistake for a school leader to lie. Fortunately, it doesn't happen often. What does happen with some frequency is a lot of educators doing a lot of denying. To the public, it's the same thing. Denying problems, failures, or mistakes that others know are real makes a leader look like a liar, a fool, or both. It's the worst communication mistake school officials can make. You can't be a believable leader and be in denial at the same time.

14. *Communication overload.* Some educators practice communication overkill. They routinely tell their audiences a lot more than they want, need, or deserve to know. There's a limit to how much listeners and readers can absorb, assimilate, and sort out. Too much information is as bad as too little. As an example, parents want to know how their kid is doing. They don't care to know all about the history of testing or the intricate norming procedures involved. The sooner that school leaders learn this lesson, the better their communication will be.

15. *Overuse of slanguage.* Some educators think that using teen slang makes them hip and strengthens communication with kids. Since the slanguage of youth changes rapidly and erratically, they also run the risk of not keeping up, misusing terms, and appearing foolish. The truth is that kids and grown-ups alike expect school leaders to talk like adults. That's why most communication experts agree that slang is most effective when used sparingly for emphasis.

16. *Showing off.* By definition, educators often have a greater-than-average vocabulary and a command of specialized terms in their discipline. Consequently, some feel a need to flaunt their vocabulary to demonstrate competence and superior knowledge and to validate their status as an authority figure. They're wrong. Using big words and exotic phrases only comes across as showing off and makes the audience less receptive to your message. Regardless of your status, using recognizable words in recognizable ways is always the best way to guarantee understanding.

17. *Being cute.* Some young educators today think that a good way to build rapport and improve communication with students is to be cute or funny. Most veteran school leaders know better. "Cute" is a tiny target. If

you shoot for it and miss, you can quickly be perceived as nerdy or pathetic. That's not the image of an effective communicator.

18. *Using profanity.* Profanity has shock value as an attention-getter, but shocking people isn't always the best way to communicate with them. When used by a school leader, profanity often embarrasses or offends people and makes it more difficult for them to take what you say seriously. Even in today's permissive society, being professional and being profane usually don't mix.

19. *Overfamiliarization.* Occasionally, school personnel make the mistake of becoming too familiar in communicating with pupils, parents, and patrons. They feel it makes them appear more chummy, accessible, and approachable. Actually, it only makes them appear out of bounds. Feigning intimacy, assuming a friendship or closeness that doesn't exist, or becoming flirtatious are things to avoid. Phony familiarity is dishonest and undermines the trust necessary for effective communication. In most cases, kids and adults have enough pals, buddies, or confidants. What they need are teachers, counselors, mentors, and leaders. That's you. Act like it.

20. *Using sexual innuendos.* Surprise! There are still some real taboos in our culture. This is one of them. Sexual hints, suggestions, and references or double entendres by school officials often make others uncomfortable and send up red flags that make effective communication difficult. It shouldn't happen in schools, but it does somewhere every day. Just check your daily newspaper for the latest story about sexual harassment in schools. Don't let it happen on your watch.

That's the list—the twenty worst communication mistakes school leaders tend to make. These aren't the only costly blunders educators are guilty of, but they are the most serious and the most common.

When you or other school leaders fail to communicate, it is usually traceable to one of these failings. Avoiding them is the first step toward saying the right thing in all school situations.

In most cases, all it takes to sidestep these pitfalls is paying attention, being honest, using plain talk, exercising common sense, showing empathy and practicing a little old-fashioned humility. If these aren't enough, the remainder of this book spells out more specifics in terms of school-tested tips, techniques, and strategies for always hitting the mark in communicating with students, parents, peers, the public, and the media. Saying the right thing in all situations isn't always easy, but it is always possible. The following pages can show you how.

Although all of the miscues above need to be addressed to ensure effective communication, some demand special attention. It should come as no surprise that hiding behind technical mumbo jumbo is one of them.

THE JARGON TRAP

Every profession has its own insider technical language. Education is no exception (see examples in Box 1.1). This jargon serves a worthwhile purpose as a shorthand or code for communicating about professional and technical topics among colleagues. It serves little or no purpose, however, for communicating with those outside the profession.

Using too much jargon can be interpreted as a sign of arrogance. Some professionals (including some educators) use it just because they can, not because it helps them communicate better. Occasionally, practitioners fall prey to the jargon trap because it makes them feel important and part of a select group.

Box 1.1   Educational Jargon: A Short List

Jargon is constantly changing as buzzwords come and go. The list below is intended only to be illustrative, not exhaustive or absolutely up-to-the-minute.

Accountability	Interdisciplinary instruction
Affective domain	Integrated learning systems
Alternative assessment techniques	Kinesthetic learning
AP classes	Learner impact statements
Assessment-driven instruction	Learner outcomes
Authentic assessment	Left brain/right brain
Block scheduling	Mainstream
Bloom's taxonomy	Management by objectives
Carnegie units	Multicultural instruction
Cognitive learning	Multisensory approach
Competency-based instruction	Norm-referenced tests
Conflict resolution training	Outcome-based education
Contract learning	Peer coaching
Cooperative learning	Percentile
Criterion-referenced tests	Postsecondary
Curriculum mapping	Profile of learning
Diagnostic teaching	Resource-based instruction
Divisional organization	Rites of passage
Emotional intelligence	Schools-within-a-school
ESL (English as a Second Language)	Scope and sequence
Flexible scheduling	Shared decision making
Focus groups	Site management
Gender-fair programs	Standard deviation
GPA (grade point average)	Strategic planning
Grade equivalent scores	Synthesis
Graduation standards	Teacher assistance teams
Homogeneous grouping	Total quality management
IEP (Individual Education Plan)	Whole language instruction
Immersion programs	Zero-based budgeting

Box 1.2   Jargon Versus Plain Talk (An Example)

Jargon: On this nationally norm-referenced standardized test, your child's score fell at the seventy-fifth percentile.

(Huh?)

Plain Talk: Your child's score was as high or higher than seventy-five percent of students the same age across the country who have taken the same test.

(Wow!)

When administrators and teachers hide behind jargon, it comes across as rude or snobbish. It doesn't work! Making people feel inferior or left out isn't a sound basis for developing mutual trust and close communication.

Using professional jargon with nonprofessionals isn't cute or clever. It's insulting, insensitive, and intimidating. If you really know what you're talking about, you can make your meaning clear without resorting to elitist jargon.

No matter who your audience members are, they deserve the truth in understandable terms, not mumbo jumbo. Effective school leaders never use "educationese" with nonprofessionals when simple words will work better. That's almost always. (See illustration in Box 1.2.)

If you have to use technical terms with pupils, parents, or patrons, be sure to define the words, explain them, give examples, and allow questions. This isn't just the best way to use jargon with people outside the profession; it's the only way.

While confusing laypeople with technical "educationese" is a major cause of miscommunication by educators, clouding issues with euphemisms may be even worse.

EUPHEMISMS FEEL GOOD, BUT DON'T SEND A CLEAR MESSAGE

Most dictionaries define *euphemism* as the "act of substituting a mild, indirect, or vague term for one considered more harsh, blunt, or offensive." Based on this definition, educators are notorious euphemizers.

When you want to be liked, admired, accepted, and respected (as most administrators and teachers do), it is difficult to be the bearer of bad news. That's why many educators resist accusing students of suspected wrongdoing. That's why they don't like to tell parents that their child acts like a jerk. That's why they are reluctant to talk about touchy topics such as physical abuse, drug use, homosexuality, or pregnancy. That's why administrators are uncomfortable when discussing sensitive personnel subjects such as an employee's drinking problem or the possibility that a teacher may be unfit for the profession.

Educators don't like to say bad things about anyone or anything, so many don't. Instead, they search for a kinder, gentler way of saying what needs to be said. They mumble. They mutter, they obfuscate. They camouflage their point with euphemisms (see Box 1.3). But hiding the truth doesn't make it go away.

The trouble with euphemisms is that they distort and dilute reality. They can leave false impressions or mislead people into thinking things are different or better than they really are. Some euphemized messages are so muted that they have no impact at all. That's not communication. It's a cop-out.

Of course, it is commendable to be considerate of others' feelings, but it's never considerate to speak or write in such vague or veiled terms that important messages don't get through. Too often euphemisms intentionally miss the mark when bull's-eyes are really needed.

The most effective school leaders aren't afraid to be honest even when it is painful or unpleasant. Problems don't get solved until someone is willing to speak frankly about them. The school's public is never well served by being deceived.

Box 1.3   Euphemisms Commonly Heard in Schools

Educators don't always say what they mean. Do you? Below are a number of euphemisms commonly heard in schools every day. If they don't sound familiar, you just may not be listening to your staff or yourself.

What Is Said:	What Is Meant:
Your child doesn't always distinguish between fact and imagination.	Your kid lies.
Your child needs improvement with motor skills and coordination.	Your child is a klutz.
Your child uses physical means to get attention or make a point.	Your child fights.
Your child has leadership skills, but needs to use them more constructively.	Your kid is a bully.
Your child lacks maturity.	He/she acts like a baby.
Your child needs more appreciation of time and punctuality.	The kid is always late.
Your child needs to develop better social skills.	Your child is gross.
Your child needs guidance in following practices of good hygiene.	Your kid is dirty.

Plain speech isn't always pretty, but it clears the air and gets the right message across. It communicates. That's what school officials are hired to do. It's fun to be Mr. Nice Guy, but it's better to be a real leader doing real communication.

When searching for the right thing to say, the best advice is to use euphemisms sparingly. Try the truth instead. It's hard to improve on honesty.

TOO MUCH POLITICAL CORRECTNESS CAN SEND WIMPY MESSAGES

In recent years, the overuse of euphemisms by school personnel has risen to almost epidemic proportions out of a growing concern over political correctness.

Modern-day Americans have gone crazy over political correctness. Educators may be even crazier than most. Whole curriculums have been purged to root out any perceived ethnic slights or slurs. Classics have been rewritten to eliminate any hint of offensive language or references. Worthwhile books have been banned because of alleged insensitive or injurious terms. Some educators are now afraid to say, write, or use anything that isn't absolutely innocuous and inoffensive. This makes communication, both in and out of the classroom, like walking through a minefield in constant fear of triggering a blowup.

Some school leaders today have become so afraid of offending minorities, protected classes, or others that they refuse to say anything that isn't 100 percent acceptable to everyone. This means that important messages often get undersaid or go unsaid altogether. We've all heard jokes about ridiculous extremes in political correctness such as referring to the bald as the "folliclely challenged." It's no joke, however, when school leaders feel they can't say what needs to be said because of paralyzing concern over political correctness. Consideration for others is good. Caution is good. Paranoia isn't.

There's a fine line between a sense of respect and a persecution complex. Too much emphasis on political correctness can lead to silly, insipid, phony, or obscured communication. Runaway political correctness neuters expression.

For example, several school leaders across the country have said they will ban Mark Twain's *Huckleberry Finn* from the curriculum because it offends some minority patrons. Sacrificing the exposure of large numbers of students to one of the greatest achievements in American literature just to satisfy the hypersensitivity of a few minority representatives is a classic illustration of excessive political correctness.

School leaders should always apply reason and fairness to what they say, but they shouldn't become so fearful of possibly offending someone that they can't communicate honestly.

Just as the best educators don't back off from touching or hugging kids who need it out of fear of sexual harassment charges, good school leaders don't forsake the truth just because they don't want to be labeled as politically incorrect. Sometimes, the right thing to say is what's real, not just what's the most politically acceptable.

How Straight Talk
Can Make You a Better School Leader

When educators fail to say the right thing, frequently the problem is that they have forgotten the power of straight talk. "Telling it like it is" still makes a difference. This means minimizing the use of jargon and euphemisms and not letting an obsessive concern with political correctness cloud essential meanings.

If you want to become a better school leader, try harder to communicate with each separate constituency at their level, using real words they understand. You may not sound as professional, Pollyannaish, or politically appropriate, but you will send clear messages. That's what counts.

When it comes to making the most of plain talk, many school leaders could take a tip from Minnesota politics. In November 1998, Jesse (The Body) Ventura, a former professional wrestler, Navy SEAL, bouncer, bodyguard for the Rolling Stones, small-town mayor, and radio personality, was elected governor of Minnesota by beating out two formidable, lifelong professional politicians.

As a first-time candidate for state office representing a low-budget third party, Ventura defeated the son of a political legend whose father was a former vice president of the United States on the Democratic ticket and a popular Republican mayor of the state's capital city. His victory wasn't a fluke, a joke, or the result of a voters' revolt. It stemmed largely from relying on straight talk.

Throughout the campaign, Ventura addressed voters in straightforward fashion using everyday language, admitting ignorance when appropriate, refusing to make promises he couldn't keep, indulging in refreshingly candid self-directed humor, speaking with honesty, and sticking to the truth.

By contrast, his opponents hedged on some touchy issues, spoke to voters using traditional political "doublespeak," relentlessly reiterated historic party lines, and came across as stuffy, self-righteous, and out of touch. (Does this sound like any educators you've ever known?)

Over time, the voters tuned out the professionals and began listening to the outsider who told it like it was in no-nonsense language, emphasizing common sense over conventional wisdom. Ventura's simple, to-the-point message was welcomed as a fresh breeze blowing through a campaign haze of politicized and polluted hot air.

Ultimately, Ventura shocked the established pundits by winning the election. Straight talk worked for Jesse Ventura. It can work for you as well. It may not get you elected to public office, but it will help you become a more effective educational leader.

What Ventura realized, which his political opponents didn't understand and too many educators forget, is that communication isn't about the sender. The purpose of effective communication isn't to make the speaker or writer sound good, look good, or feel good. It's about being understood and believed by the receivers.

When administrators and teachers tell it like it is using language that is readily understood, students learn more, follow directions better, and are more likely to make positive behavior changes. Likewise, parents become more willing and effective partners with the school because they understand what's going on and why; the public supports the school with greater vigor because it really hears and grasps the school's message; and the media treat the school fairly, because reporters feel they are dealt with honestly.

Straight talk makes a difference because it saves time, eliminates confusion, builds trust, and establishes credibility. Best of all, it is understood and believed! This makes straight talk too good a deal for you and other school leaders to miss out on.

Learning to communicate plainly and honestly is a key to professional success for school leaders. Knowing the right thing to say in every situation isn't magic. It's not a gift. It's a trait that can be acquired only through conscious effort and hard work. Straight talk is more than borrowing someone else's words. It is a skill developed by steadfastly searching for the simplest and sincerest way to communicate in your own words to a variety of specific audiences.

The skill of plain talk is rooted in an understanding of what works and what doesn't in getting across to students, parents, co-workers, the public, and the media. It means making it a habit to make your point clear.

The strategies laid out in the following chapters can give you all the necessary tips and tools to become a better straight-talk communicator, no matter what audience or situation you are dealing with. When that happens, you will have become a better school leader at the same time.

WHEN THE RIGHT THING TO SAY IS "NOTHING"

While embracing the value of straight talk, school personnel also need to realize often there is one communication tool that is even more powerful and effective: no talk at all.

We all know administrators and teachers who believe they are perpetually obligated to say something. They feel compelled to always make a point, teach a lesson, or impart "wisdom" (whatever that is). Unfortunately, they are missing the point of communication. It's supposed to be two-way. More often than most of us think, "nothing" is the right thing to say. Silence often speaks louder than words.

It is no secret that a lot of educators tend to talk too much. Every day, all school leaders have countless opportunities to shut up. The best make the most of all of them. Listening is the unspoken secret to successful communication. You can never learn to say the right thing every time until you learn to really listen first. Examples of common situations when nothing is the best way to communicate include

- When you don't fully understand what is expected
- When the other person is merely venting feelings, not seeking information or advice
- When all that's needed is support, not feedback
- When you are angry or otherwise unable to remain objective
- When you don't know what to say
- When you've already said too much

When weighing what to say, it always pays to remember that the clearest, most long-lasting, and best-remembered messages are those that people discover for themselves.

MORE "MUST-DO" TIPS FOR ALWAYS SAYING THE RIGHT THING

Whether it is avoiding jargon, eschewing euphemisms, or just "listening up" more, becoming a better communicator is not a matter of a major makeover. Improvement is incremental, resulting from simply learning to do a lot of little things just a little bit better.

Examples include the following steps that have helped many successful school leaders learn how to say the right thing. They can help you as well. They all work. They're all doable. But they won't make any difference unless you apply them. The best time to start is now:

- Remember that when you communicate with students, you are the adult. When you communicate with adults, keep in mind that you are the professional. Your words should match your role. (The Bible has it right—"When I was a child, I spake as a child. When I became a man, I put away childish ways.")

- Tailor your communication to specific listeners or readers. Communication must be audience-appropriate to be effective.
- Take a tip from the Golden Rule. Communicate with people the way you want to be communicated with.
- Don't worry too much about maintaining the image or mystique of what you think an educator is supposed to be or sound like. Talk like a real person. Real people in your audience will appreciate it.
- If you can't be anything else, be clear. The gift of a good leader or teacher is the ability to make complex subjects clear, simple, understandable, and less intimidating. Effectiveness is not measured by the quantity of polysyllabic words used, but by how much of what is said or written is really understood.
- Talk *to* people, not *at* them.
- Shy away from sarcasm, put-downs, insults, and name-calling. Cheap shots are almost always costly.
- Don't say anything that you (and your audience) know is phony.
- Remember the power of civility. If they cause you to become angry, you lose your audience even if it's only one person.
- Lighten up and tighten up. Don't take yourself too seriously and don't drone on and on!
- Give real reasons for action, not just policy references.
- Answer the questions that are really asked, not just the ones you want to answer.
- Make sure that your mouth, your eyes, and your body are all saying the same thing.
- Be consistent. Tell all groups the same thing—but in ways that are most meaningful to each individual constituency.
- Remove physical and psychological barriers between you and your audience. Get out from behind the desk. Look at your audience. Lean toward your audience. Get as close as you can—just don't get in their face.

- Get to the point.
- Follow the "KISS" principal advocated by AA— "Keep It Simple, Stupid."
- Be respectful. It's the only way to earn respect yourself.
- In all you say or write, remember that shorter is better.
- Remember that half-truths are also half-lies. Avoid them.
- Say what needs to be said as soon as you can possibly say it! Read this again. It may be the single most important guiding principle for school leaders who want to be better communicators.
- If what you have to say doesn't add anything, don't say it.
- Listen to yourself. If you don't like what you hear, do something about it.
- Listen to how the leaders you admire most express themselves. Emulate what works. There is no copyright on saying the right thing.
- Dare to be passionate about your values, beliefs, priorities, and what you stand for. Passion is persuasive.
- If it doesn't feel right, don't say it.

If you have ever had trouble knowing what to say to students, parents, or the public, the starter suggestions above can help you avoid similar embarrassment in the future. And it keeps getting better.

Each of the following chapters contains more specific guidelines, models, suggestions, and school-tested examples to equip you to communicate effectively with all groups in all situations. It starts by understanding how to get through to today's students.

2

How to Say the Right Thing to Students

As a school leader, you have to communicate with kids. That's your job. You have to be able to speak and write so that students will really listen (or read), accept, understand, believe, remember, and act on what you say. In and out of the classroom, instructions must be clear, messages straight to the point, and meanings understandable, or nothing else you do matters very much.

Unfortunately, getting through to today's students isn't always easy. (If it were, anybody could be a principal or teacher.) Kids can be a tough audience. Even the best school leaders sometimes get stuck in situations where they don't know what to say or how to say it in order to make their point or get their message across to kids.

It doesn't have to be that way. Saying the right thing to students in all situations is a skill that can be learned. Even the best communicators can learn to be more effective. It starts by understanding exactly what works and what doesn't when communicating with today's children and youth.

Good communication with students is often rooted in a shared history. It develops incrementally over time through a track record of trust, mutual respect, rapport, and credibility. When school leaders consistently listen to students, take them seriously, tell the truth, keep promises, and respect feelings, young people are much more likely to really listen to what they say and to respond positively.

The odds in favor of effective communication with kids are increased even more when school personnel follow certain commonsense principles.

TEN GUIDELINES FOR COMMUNICATING WITH STUDENTS

Intergenerational communication is always tricky. Adults and kids have different background experiences, perspectives, vocabulary, interests, priorities, and agendas. Nevertheless, there are special approaches and considerations that can help bridge the generation gap:

Ten Guidelines for Communicating With Students

1. Talk to students the way you want them to talk to you. (The Golden Rule still works.)

2. Think before you speak or write. What you say to children can become a self-fulfilling prophecy.

3. Remember that how you say something to students is as important as what you say.

4. To avoid sounding judgmental, stick to describing what you see and feel.

5. Encourage students to share personal thoughts and feelings by sharing your own. (Self-disclosure opens up communication.)

6. Never use words to belittle any child's dreams.

7. Show by what you say and how you say it that you take students (and their problems and feelings) seriously.

8. If you show that you enjoy listening to students, they will be more likely to listen to you.

9. When communicating verbally with students, the smaller the group, the better. One-on-one is best. Break large groups into smaller ones when giving complicated instructions.

10. Be willing to talk about whatever kids really want to talk about.

Sticking to these strategies may not guarantee effective communication with students, but ignoring them is a surefire recipe for failure and misunderstanding. It also pays to remember that straight talk is never more important than when relating to children and youth.

STRAIGHT TALK IS THE LANGUAGE OF CHOICE WITH KIDS

There are lots of ways to communicate with students. Many of them don't work. Just ask the parents of any teenager. Better yet, ask the teenager. Fortunately, however, getting through to today's kids doesn't have to be as complicated as many adults make it.

The best way to get through to students is simply to say what you mean and what needs to be said in plain language and at the earliest appropriate time. (This should come as no surprise, because this is the best way to communicate with all age groups.) When it comes to communicating with kids, straight talk beats adultspeak, jargon, shock talk, street talk, slang, or phony "studentese" every time.

Younger students don't understand the polite double-talk that characterizes much of adult conversation. Older students have no patience for it. Likewise, using professional jargon or technical terms may work when educators communicate with each other, but it doesn't mean a thing to kids. They just think you are showing off.

Trying to shock or scare students doesn't work either and usually falls on deaf ears. Using too much slang only trivializes important messages and turns kids off. Likewise, affecting street talk or the latest teen culture code words can easily make you appear ridiculous.

Students expect straight talk from their school leaders. Give it to them. It works!

If you want to reach students through what you say or by what you put in writing,

- Don't lie to or mislead them.
- Don't talk over their heads.
- Talk directly to them in words they understand.

All good administrators and teachers have known this all along, but sometimes forget or get out of the habit, because it's easier and more comfortable to be vague and noncommittal. The lesson of straight talk is worth remembering, no matter what age group you're dealing with.

HOW TO TALK TO YOUNG CHILDREN ON THEIR LEVEL

Talking to little kids is different—but not as different or difficult as many adults (even some educators) make it (see Box 2.1).

Even very young children know more and understand a lot more than they are often given credit for.

Of course, using a lot of big, grown-up words won't work with small children. Neither will slathering on a lot of baby talk. Acting interested and being honest, approachable, and respectful will.

What's most different about little kids is that they (a) have a short attention span, (b) are easily distracted, (c) are brutally honest, (d) say what they feel, and (e) tend to believe what adults tell them (at least, until we teach them otherwise).

To handle these differences, get and hold their attention, and get through to young children on their level, it pays to do the following:

- Start by listening. Really listening. Not just paying lip service to listening.
- Talk to the students, not at them.
- Accept and reflect what children tell you they are feeling.
- Help them find a name for their feelings (i.e., fear, embarrassment, jealousy, anger, happiness).
- Remember that how you say it is as important as what you say. Plenty of smiles and eye contact will buy a lot of attentive listening time from little kids.

Box 2.1   What to Avoid When Talking to Small Children

AVOID:	Screaming	Threatening
	Yelling	Teasing
	Name calling	Exploiting
	Blaming	Belittling
	Shaming	Nagging
	Swearing	Insulting

(Surprise! The same rules apply when talking to big kids as well.)

Good elementary teachers and principals do all of these things naturally. Secondary and district personnel and other adults often need a little help to become comfortable communicating with very young students.

Other insider tips that work with elementary-age students include the following:

- Take a page from the elementary teachers' handbook and literally get down on their level in order to get through to young children. Kneeling, crouching, sitting, and leaning forward to get closer to your audience makes it easier to communicate with little kids. Proximity promotes understanding and acceptance.
- Radiate confidence (even if you don't feel it).
- Stick to simple language and concrete terms.
- Be animated. Use props whenever possible.
- Use lots of action words and colorful language.
- Check frequently for understanding. Watch the faces. Nodding heads mean understanding. Wandering eyes and a glazed-over expression show you've lost them. Repeatedly ask for a show of hands or insert questions to determine if students are tuned in.

Don't press fiercely forward if the children are obviously not getting it. Getting through your material isn't what's important. Getting through to the students is.

- Avoid clichés and phrases that turn kids off, such as, "You're too young to understand" or the dreaded, "This hurts me more than it hurts you." (Kids have never believed this one.)
- Be upbeat, encouraging, and optimistic. Kids always respond to enthusiasm.
- Limit the number of times you say "no."
- Restate problems as questions. If that doesn't work, rephrase the questions.
- Don't rush to provide answers or fill in periods of silence.

- Avoid sarcasm or saying anything that might embarrass a little child.
- Don't exaggerate too much. Little kids are liable to believe you.
- If you start to lose your audience, remain calm. Don't keep talking louder and louder. You can't out-shout them. Instead, decrease your volume to regain attention.

Following these steps will help educators or any adult say the right thing every time to little children. It's easier than many people think. Best of all, it's more fun than talking to grown-ups. And it's often a piece of cake, compared to interacting with teenagers.

How to Talk to Today's Teenagers

Teenagers have a razor-sharp bullshit detector.

—Kenny Loggins

Who's afraid to talk to today's teenagers? Almost every adult, including some of their parents. Talking to teens can be like traversing a verbal minefield. It may blow up in your face any time. But it doesn't have to be that way.

Contrary to a popular misconception, teenagers aren't aliens or ogres. They're just people like all the rest of us—with certain common distinguishing characteristics:

- They love to shock.
- They love to criticize what adults do, say, think, and write.
- They are impatient and in a hurry for answers and solutions.
- They are both cynical and idealistic at the same time—just like all previous generations of adolescents.
- They are self-absorbed, hypersensitive to critics, and easily embarrassed. ("Having taught teens . . . I know

with some certainty that to them, everything is embarrassing." —Renee Rosenblum-Lowden)

- They use a lot of words and phrases that would have been offensive or taboo in their parents' teen years.
- They want independence and freedom to grow, but also appreciate boundaries and direction provided by caring adults.
- They hate phoniness, stereotypes, labels, inconsistency, double standards, and hypocrisy.

The ever-present critics of today's teenagers might be surprised to see that there is a lot more on this list to admire than to castigate.

Once professionals, parents, and other adults understand the general traits of adolescence and remember what it was like to be a teenager, finding the right thing to say to teens is usually no longer a big problem. If that's not enough help, the additional guidelines below will go a long way toward ensuring that your spoken or written messages are accepted as credible and believable by teenagers:

- Be authentic. Do what you say you're going to do. (Walk your talk.) Don't waffle or weasel out of answering tough questions. (The principle of straight talk just won't go away.) This is particularly true when dealing with at-risk behavior such as alcohol, drugs, and sex.
- Dare to talk about your values. Passion is persuasive. Teenagers resonate to adults who stand for something.
- Be absolutely clear about expectations. Have reasons for your rules. And consistently follow through with predetermined consequences.
- Strive to be nonjudgmental. Avoid absolutes such as "always" or "never."
- Don't try to con kids. It won't work. They are probably better at it than you are anyway.

- Ask lots of how and why questions.
- Don't personalize the need teens have to test limits and rebel against authority.
- Be stingy with advice.
- Don't patronize or sermonize.
- Concentrate on the present and future, not the past. Don't dwell on past mistakes. Practice amnesty and be willing to give lots of second chances.
- Don't trivialize ideas or issues that are important to students.
- Avoid offering simplistic solutions.
- Don't come across as a martyr. Kids don't care. Live with it. (If you invite teens to your pity party, they won't show up.)
- Don't try to talk like a teenager to get through to teenagers. It won't work. They know you're a school leader. You should too. Act like it.
- Respect student privacy and confidentiality (within legal limits).
- Be scrupulous in avoiding any perception of over-familiarity with students. Steer clear of off-color language, profanity, double entendres, or sexual references.
- When teens are down, remind them of the good times and assure them that there will be lots of good times ahead.

If you follow these steps and it still doesn't work, don't back off. Persist. Keep trying to get your point across. Teenagers are used to having people give up on them. Don't be a fair-weather friend.

If you keep showing up, you will eventually get through to even the most reticent, resistant, or rebellious teenager. And it won't make any difference if it's a girl or a boy.

Differences in Talking to Boys and Girls

Americans have made a big deal out of differences in communication styles between the sexes. We've all been made aware of the variations in the way men and women process information, express feelings, and interpret meanings. So what does all that mean for school leaders trying to communicate with students on a daily basis? Not much!

Men may come from Mars and women from Venus, but kids seem to be essentially from the same planet. When it comes to communication in school, there appear to be few substantive differences between students of the opposite sex. They are more alike than different. We've always known that. It's still true—particularly at the elementary level. The younger the students, the fewer the differences.

The good news is that educators don't have to develop separate vocabularies or strategies for communicating with male and female students. Basically, what works in getting through to boys, works in getting across to girls as well.

There is probably some advantage in using traditional masculine examples (e.g., sports) with boys and traditional feminine references (e.g., fashions) with girls, but this is not a major consideration.

Internalized cultural differences do begin to kick in or become more pronounced at the secondary level. Even here, however, the differences are getting blurred as the opportunities and experiences for boys and girls become more parallel.

For example, more and more girls are now participating in athletics, even in sports formerly reserved exclusively for boys, such as hockey. Consequently, sports metaphors, which used to pass right over most girls' heads, are now meaningful to both sexes.

Nevertheless, there are still a few distinctions in the way boys and girls handle communication that school leaders need to deal with, including the following:

- Boys are ordinarily more literal in communicating than girls. Boys tend to mean exactly what they say and often incorrectly assume that everybody else does too. Contrarily, girls are more prone to exaggerate, make sweeping generalizations, and use superlatives.

- Girls use more "rapport talk" (talk that helps make connection and build relationships), while boys engage in more "report talk" (talk designed to provide information and solve problems).

- When upset, boys tend to clam up, while girls are more likely to talk about their feelings.

- Boys hate pity and sometimes confuse expressions of empathy for signs of sympathy, and they don't like it. Boys are also more likely than girls to equate complaining with blaming.

- When boys nod at what you are saying, they usually mean agreement. Girls nod only to indicate they are hearing what you are saying, not necessarily that they agree with it.

- Girls commonly think out loud. It's a way to share their thought processes. Boys tend to think to themselves and then tell you what they have concluded.

- Girls are generally more uncomfortable with silence and often talk just to fill the void. Boys shut up more.

- In adolescence, boys frequently use cleverly barbed put-downs to help teach each other how to handle criticism. When girls use put-downs, they usually mean it.

None of these differences is likely to be a deal-breaker when communicating with kids, but knowing about them may explain some past communication lapses and make sending and receiving messages easier for your students in the future.

What is more important to remember about communicating across generations and to both sexes is that the devil is in the detail. It's not a matter of mastering a few fundamentals or doing a few things right. It's about doing lots of little things right. It means paying attention to all the details (do's and don'ts) that kids notice and that matter to them.

ANOTHER DOZEN DO'S AND DON'TS FOR SAYING THE RIGHT THING TO KIDS OF ALL AGES

Although there is no foolproof formula, the following specific proactive measures and cautions (do's and don'ts) can make communicating with students of any age easier, more effective, more efficient, and a lot more fun:

Do's

- Listen more than you talk.
- Use students' names to get their attention.
- Acknowledge that growing up isn't easy.
- Personalize communication to students when possible.
- Use metaphors to clarify.
- Give students your undivided attention.
- Stick to facts.
- Take enough time to get your message across.
- Show that you care.
- Search for language that boosts students' self-esteem.
- Speak loudly enough so that even the kids in the back row can hear.
- Be the adult!

Don'ts

- Give long-winded explanations.
- Talk more about yourself than about others.
- Try to bluff students.
- Knowingly lie to students (or adults).
- Jump to conclusions.
- Use flirtatious or suggestive language.
- Accuse without proof.
- Say anything to take away any student's hope.
- Make a habit of telling students a lot more than they want or need to know.
- Intimidate students.

- Soft-pedal bad news because you think kids can't handle the truth.
- Take your words or yourself too seriously.

It seems almost too good to be true, but it isn't. If you take care of the minor details in communicating, the big stuff will take care of itself. That's why saying the right thing to today's kids every time is a lot easier than many people believe. This is never more true than when giving "must-understand" instructions or explanations.

How to Give Clear Directions and Instructions Every Time

Many people think giving directions or instructions is easy. After all, it's just telling someone what to do and how to do it. They're wrong.

If instruction giving were easy, there wouldn't be so many students who chronically don't know what they are supposed to do or don't have a clue as to how to do it. If the kids don't "get it," they can't do it. How many times have students been confused by your directions?

Even adults often have difficulty with directions. For many people, the popular phrase "easy-to-follow instructions" is an oxymoron. Most of those who claim that giving and following instructions are easy probably haven't looked at their computer's user manual for a while.

The key to giving confusion-proof instructions is to follow the KISS model. KISS stands for "Keep It Simple, Stupid." According to this model, you can't make instructions too simple. It's better to dumb down directions than to have them go unread, unused, or misunderstood.

Directions always work best if they are conveyed in a variety of modalities (visual, auditory, and tactile) so that pupils can receive them in the way that is more compatible with their preferred learning style or method of processing information.

It also pays to take a tip from TV commercials. Don't be afraid to repeat yourself. Repetition is the mother of understanding. Never assume that everyone "gets it" the first time. As long as one student doesn't understand or is unable to follow the directions, you're not done yet. Many advertisers suggest that a message be repeated at least four times before most people internalize it. What works for TV can work in your school as well.

Other surefire steps that many successful school leaders use to ensure giving simple, clear, and accurate instructions every time include the following:

- Get everyone's attention before you begin giving instructions. Real pros don't start until everyone is listening. It may take a while, but the wait is worth it.
- Don't give too many instructions at once. Break them down into manageable, understandable tasks (small incremental steps).
- If the instructions are written, number the steps and use diagrams or flow charts if appropriate (see sample directions in Box 2.2).
- Use concrete words and straightforward sentences. No convoluted sentence structure allowed.
- Avoid the temptation to use technical terms. If you have to use them, be sure to define each term with familiar words.
- Be specific. Be consistent. Be complete.
- Go slowly.
- Explain "why" as well as "how" to do it.
- Check frequently for understanding.
- Supplement verbal instructions by demonstrating how to do it when practical. This helps all the visual learners in the group.
- Avoid condescending language such as, "This is so simple any fool can do it."
- Word instructions positively. Just tell the learners what to do, not all the things they shouldn't do.

Box 2.2   Sample Instructions

Assignment Sheet for Social Studies 8

What: Writing assignment. Write a 500- to 800-word paper on the history and causes of today's Middle East conflict between Israel and Palestine.

Why: To develop better understanding of current events and the factors contributing to misunderstandings between nations.

When: The deadline is October 15.

How: a. Gather information from three (3) credible sources. Don't rely totally on the Internet, where some information is not verifiable.

b. Organize and outline your paper. Let the teacher review and comment on your outline.

c. Prepare a rough draft.

d. Polish, refine, and rewrite a final draft.

e. Be sure to list complete information identifying your sources.

f. Type or word process the final draft.

g. Proofread your final draft carefully. Don't rely solely on any spell-checking computer program. Get a second person to help proofread if necessary.

h. Hand in *on time.*

Don't be afraid to ask questions at any time during the assignment period.

Giving good instructions is a measure of effectiveness. If you can't give clear directions, you can't be a successful school leader.

There are only three possible causes for the misunderstanding of instructions:

1. The sender

2. The message

3. The receiver

As the educator-in-charge, you control two out of three variables. Make sure there is no confusion about directions on your watch. If it's not in your job description, it should be.

As with most student communication, straight talk is the basis for issuing clear instructions. It's also the foundation for asking good questions.

SOCRATES HAD IT RIGHT:
HOW TO ASK EFFECTIVE QUESTIONS

Sometimes asking the right question is more important than saying the right thing. Socrates revealed his most significant lessons through questioning. Effective school leaders do the same. They also use adroit questioning to find out what students really know, understand, feel, and think. The only way to get thoughtful, honest answers from students is to ask good questions.

Good questions often make a statement. The kind of questions you ask says a lot about what you value. Shallow questions tell students that you're not really interested, you don't care too much, and/or the subject matter isn't very important. Conversely, reflective questions can show your deeper interests, concerns, and priorities.

Students don't ask dumb questions. Administrators and teachers do. If you want to find out anything worthwhile, don't waste time on questions that don't matter. To avoid asking dumb questions, stay away from trick questions; confusing questions; "yes" and "no" questions; ambiguous questions; obvious-answer questions; closed questions (which have only one narrow answer); or recital questions (which call only for memorized responses).

Box 2.3   Examples of Big-Payoff Questions

What other solutions are there?
What other uses can you think of?
How could it be done differently?
Describe_____and compare it to_____.
What else?
What if?
And the most important questions of all:
Why? Or Why not?

To challenge your students and find out what they really know or think, ask the kind of questions that yield the biggest payoffs (see Box 2.3). Experienced educators usually get the best results by asking:

- "How" and "why" questions:
  1. Open questions (which have more than one possible answer)
  2. Dialogue questions (which require some reflection or deeper thought)
  3. Divergent questions (which require thinking about new possibilities)

Other school-tested tips that can help any school leader ask the right questions include the following:

- Have a reason for any question you ask.
- Keep your questions clean and clear.
- Start with easier and narrower questions and progress to broader and more difficult ones.
- Don't ask the questions everyone else is asking.
- Ask the questions you really want answered. (Kids do this naturally all the time, but adults tend to hedge on edgy issues.)
- Stay away from asking personal questions.
- Be willing to answer your own questions.
- Don't ask questions just to look good.
- Don't call on a specific respondent too soon. It lets everyone else off the hook too easily.
- Allow enough "wait time." Don't rush for a response. Practice patience. Silence is OK if it eventually makes students uncomfortable enough to respond.
- Try some speculative questions.
- If responses aren't forthcoming, restate, rephrase, or reframe the question.
- Always probe beyond the initial response.
- You can multiply the effectiveness of any question by asking the respondent to clarify or elaborate.

- Don't interrupt any student's answer.
- Pay close attention to incorrect answers. Wrong responses can tell you what students don't know and why they don't know it.
- Don't cross-examine students.
- Recognize overkill. Don't ask too many questions. It's time to move on when answers start to be repeated.

Good questions save time and get the right people talking and thinking. One effective question can be worth a half-dozen lectures. Often, the best way to get your message across is to let your students find it in the answers they give to carefully crafted questions. That's why it pays to spend as much time drafting your questions as you do anything else you say or write.

How to Give Students "Pep Talks" That Really Work

Surprise! Even coaches need pep talks. Everyone does. Kids do most of all. Sooner or later, every school leader has to find the right words to help students rebound from disappointment and get geared up to try again.

Everyone has a down time sometimes when they need an encouraging word or a verbal kick in the pants. It's called a pep talk, and it's one of the things effective school leaders do best.

We can learn about pep talks from the inspirational rhetoric of legendary coaches such as Knute Rockne or Vince Lombardi, but we can't learn very much. The old clichés (e.g., "Win one for the Gipper" or "When the going gets tough, the tough get going") aren't so effective anymore. Bombastic exhortations don't work so well either. Today's kids are too sophisticated for some of the old approaches.

What does work is straight talk about possibilities, hope, building on strengths, and the power of second efforts. Whether it's bolstering a flagging athletic team or urging a frustrated student to keep working, simple encouragement works better than off-the-wall theatrics.

The purpose of any pep talk is to motivate, rejuvenate, and offer support—not to add more pressure. Good pep talks don't browbeat, threaten, intimidate, or embarrass. It's hard to scare people (even young people) into overcoming adversity. What works better is a straightforward approach built around the following ten guidelines:

1. Encourage small steps and incremental improvement.

2. Avoid ridiculous overstatements.

3. Remind students that good things are still possible.

4. Use lots of empowering words and phrases (see Box 2.4).

5. Use "descriptive praise." Point out specific examples of things the student has done in the past that will prepare him or her for success in the future.

6. Emphasize that the best response to setback is renewed effort.

7. Avoid platitudes and obvious exaggerations.

8. Mean what you say.

9. Cite positive examples of real people the student knows.

10. Celebrate effort, not just outcomes.

Most people normally think of pep talks as presentations to large groups, but in real life, the most important ones are delivered one-on-one, eyeball-to-eyeball by someone who cares. In these situations, simple and sincere beats ranting and raving every time. You can't encourage by innuendo or pussyfooting around in a pep talk. Instead, be positive. Be enthusiastic. Be emphatic. And be clear!

You don't have to be a great orator to deliver pep talks that work with today's students, but you do have to be willing to demonstrate unconditional caring, pledge unflinching support, and use plain talk that leaves no doubt that things can get better.

Box 2.4   Empowering Words and Phrases

Effort	Success
Commitment	Fresh start
Winning	Worthwhile
Support	Celebrate
Advantage	Confidence
Special	Support
Choice	It gets easier.
Achieve	You're not alone.
Reward	We're in your corner.
Second chance	One step at a time.
You can do it.	People will help.
People care what we do.	You deserve it.
Do it for yourself.	You're stronger than you think you are.
You can be proud of . . .	Pride
You've done it before.	Help
We believe in you.	Goals
"Failure is an event, not a person."	Payoff
(—Zig Ziglar)	Encourage
Teamwork	Possible
Future	Breakthrough
Victory	Growth
Triumph	Faith

HOW TO GIVE AUTHENTIC PRAISE

Honest praise is essential for positive student growth and development. Of all the messages we send to students, praise is the most important. It can set standards, reinforce desired behavior, challenge, motivate, and build self-confidence. That's why it's critical to do it right.

On the surface, praising a child would seem to be a simple and natural act. What could be easier? Nevertheless, adults (including school leaders) often can and do screw it up.

When praise is bungled, it can do more harm than good. False praise, like inflated grades, is a hollow promise. Instead of setting students up for success, it sets them up for rude awakenings, disappointment, and failure by creating unfounded perceptions and distorted expectations. Worst of all, kids can become dependent on receiving praise they don't earn or deserve. This is the greatest disservice adults can do for children.

Mishandled, praise is a cruel hoax. It can damage the credibility of the school leader who gives it. Even worse, it can appear threatening or intimidating, create anxiety, trigger denial, and feel like manipulation. Unfounded, unrealistic, or inappropriate praise is worse than no praise at all.

Whether you give it in public or private, put it in a note or jot it on a student's paper, if you want praise to be effective, it pays to follow a few simple student-tested do's and don'ts:

Rules for Praise

Do's

- Be honest. Kids spot phony praise every time. ("Kids know bull from real." —Judge Judy)
- Make praise age appropriate. Praise doesn't work if the child doesn't understand it. Gild the lily.
- Be specific. "Descriptive praise" is always the best praise. Describe exactly why the student is being praised. Summarize what is praiseworthy about it.

Don'ts

- Mix praise with criticism.
- Make a bigger deal out of the situation than it deserves. Kids know exaggeration when they see it.
- Act surprised that the student achieved or excelled. The idea is to show confidence in the young person, not to convey skepticism or doubt.

Praise (Box 2.5) is the currency of teaching and educational leadership, but the only worthwhile praise is authentic praise. Anything less is counterfeit. The goal of authentic praise is to help students realize what's right about themselves.

When delivered honestly in clear-cut terms, praise works better than fault finding for improving student self-esteem, behavior, effort, and performance. It's too good a tool for school leaders to ignore or misuse.

HOW TO HELP KIDS TALK THEMSELVES INTO SUCCESS

Praise is powerful, heady stuff, especially when it comes from inside. Contrary to popular wisdom, you don't have to be crazy to talk to yourself. We all do it. This is a good thing.

What we say to ourselves about ourselves largely determines who we are and how we do in life. Somebody needs to tell kids about this. It's one of the "right things" to say to students.

What adults say to kids shapes their perceptions and performance. What peers say to them affects their self-confidence and behavior even more. But the internal dialogue kids have with themselves has the greatest impact of all. Believe it or not, students can talk themselves into success. You can help.

Positive self-talk can become a self-fulfilling prophecy. Of course, it can work exactly in reverse if self-talk is negative. If kids (or adults) bad-mouth themselves long enough and hard enough, they can become their own worst enemies and end up hating themselves and others. This may be what happened at Columbine High School.

Box 2.5a Ways to Praise

There are lots of ways to praise. It comes in many forms—verbal, written, and nonverbal. Here are 100 common examples of popular praise phrases and signals that work with today's students.	
Great job.	Take a bow.
Congratulations.	You did it.
Outstanding work.	YES!
Awesome.	Your best ever.
That was great.	I'm impressed.
You're #1.	Wow.
Super.	Excellent.
Wonderful work.	Much better.
Terrific.	Tremendous. *(continued)*

Box 2.5b Ways to Praise *(continued)*

You did it just right.	First-class work.
A singular accomplishment.	You surpassed your goal.
Take your place in the winner's circle.	A blue-ribbon success.
Cool!	Look how far you've come.
A-1 work.	Remarkable.
Fantastic.	Spectacular.
We're proud of you.	Magnificent.
That's your personal best.	Right on!
Superior.	Far out!
Fabulous.	I can't believe it.
Excellent.	You came through.
Fine work.	Top rate.
Well done.	Perfect.
Amazing.	Bull's-eye!
You should feel good about it.	This is your moment.
You hit the top of the charts.	You made a believer out of everyone.
A beautiful job.	A winning effort.
You aced it.	You even surprised yourself.
A real breakthrough.	What an achievement.
You earned it.	Better than expected.
Another triumph.	You broke your own record.
We knew you could do it.	A well-deserved honor.
You blew away the competition.	In a class by yourself.
Marvelous.	Stupendous.
Hooray!	Cheers!
Brilliant performance.	Above average.
You showed everyone.	A-OK.
Another milestone.	A mighty effort.
Couldn't be better.	Off the charts.
You deserve a standing ovation.	I love it.
You knocked their socks off.	One for the record books.
Humungous.	Unreal!
You left 'em in the dust.	You make it look easy.
Award-winning.	A class act.
Pat yourself on the back.	You proved yourself.

Not all effective praise is expressed in words. Some of the most powerful praise is conveyed nonverbally. Here's how:

Thumbs up	High fives
Applause	Hugs
Smiles	Nods
Handshakes	Winks
OK sign	V for Victory sign

One way to make sure this doesn't occur is for students to feed themselves positive self-talk. Successful performers in all fields start each day by reciting self-affirming mental messages. It may sound silly at first, but it makes a difference. It's a way to boost self-confidence, validate self-worth, and prepare for what each day brings. It's a means for kids to become their own best cheerleaders. School leaders can (and should) make it happen in three important ways:

1. Set kids up for success by giving them lots of positive experiences to talk to themselves about.

2. Teach kids about the power of self-talk. Give them examples (see Box 2.6).

3. Give students permission (power) to manage their own self-talk. Teach them that they can change their lives by restating their self-affirmations.

Box 2.6   Examples of Positive Student Self-Affirmations

I am enough.

I'm okay.

I'm getting better.

I can do the right thing.

God isn't done with me yet. He has plans for me.

I'm mature enough to make healthy choices.

Lots of people care about me and want me to succeed.

I have the right stuff.

I have the right to say "no."

I am a miracle.

Nothing and no one controls me.

I'm working on my faults. I'm becoming a better person.

The best is yet to come for me.

I'm going to surprise the world.

God, I look good!

While learning to say the right thing to students in all situations, take time to help kids learn to say the right thing to themselves. Self-affirmations are easy. They're free. And they work. Let kids in on the secret. It's a way to help students help themselves.

RHETORIC-FREE REPRIMANDS

When school leaders have to bawl out a student, it is no time for evasion, double-talk, or fancy word tricks. Discipline requires a straightforward, clear-cut message. No frills. A reprimand shouldn't be a hint, a suggestion, or an innuendo, and students shouldn't have to guess the meaning.

When issuing a verbal or written reprimand, forget the unnecessary rhetoric. Don't waste words. The best reprimand is a sentence, not a sermon.

Sometimes, weak administrators and teachers compound their discipline problems because they can't bring themselves to say what has to be said. Instead, they obfuscate and talk around the subject. They don't want to hurt anyone's feelings, risk an unpleasant confrontation, or be perceived as overly mean or harsh. Conversely, the best school leaders make their point without personalizing it and move on. Boom. It's over. No aftertaste.

If you want to issue no-nonsense, rhetoric-free reprimands that stick, the following tips can help:

- Take reprimanding seriously. This is not the time to be flippant or nonchalant.
- Don't procrastinate, waffle, or hem and haw. Get straight to the point. Just do it!
- Never apologize for reprimanding a student. You are not the one who should feel sorry.
- Don't even think about saying, "This will hurt me more than it hurts you."
- Choose the best time and the right setting.
- Choose your words carefully (see examples in Box 2.7).

Box 2.7   The Language of Reprimand

Action	Failure	Probation
Advice	Fair	Problem
Against policy	Fault	Punishment
Allegation	Felony	Reasonable effort
Amends	Fines	Record
Antisocial	Good faith	Recourse
Apologize	Hearing	Repetition
Authority	Illegal	Reputation
Bad judgment	Immaturity	Resolution
Behavior	Inappropriate	Responsibility
Below expectations	Indefensible	Restraining order
Boundaries	Inexcusable	Rights
Charges	Intolerable	Rules
Common sense	Judgment	Solution
Complaint	Judicial	Standards
Conduct	Juvenile	Suspect
Consent	Lack of	Terroristic
Consequences	Laws	Testimony
Consistent	Lawyer	Threats
Counsel	Limits	Unacceptable
Courtesy	Litigation	Unbecoming
Courts	Lying	Unfortunate
Criminal	Misdemeanor	Unlawful
Damage	Misinterpreted	Unpleasant
Delinquent	Misjudged	Unsatisfactory
Disappointed	Negative attitude	Upset
Discipline	Offenses	Victim
Duty	Off-limits	Violation
Effort	Options	Witnessed
Embarrassment	Prohibited	Wrong
Evidence	Property damage	Zero tolerance
Excuses	Payback	

- Match the intensity of the reprimand to the severity of the offense.
- Focus on behaviors, not personalities. Express disapproval without attacking the student's character.
- Don't just say the words. Look the look. Eye contact makes all the difference.
- Be accurate, firm, clear, honest, and direct.
- Never reprimand in anger. Professionalism and vindictiveness don't mix.

- Remember that discipline should be more about learning than about punishment. Improved behavior is always the goal.
- Avoid sarcasm. It comes across as a cheap shot.
- Avoid overkill.
- If the reprimand is written (see sample letter in Box 2.8), resist the temptation to be overly formal or to write like a lawyer. Educators write to get their point across. Lawyers write to stay out of trouble.

Box 2.8   Sample Letter of Reprimand*

Dear_____:

This letter Is an official reprimand for your unacceptable behavior during the basketball game on Friday, January 13. Several students and teachers witnessed your unprovoked physical assault on a younger student during halftime of the game. Although no one was seriously injured, fighting at any school event is explicitly prohibited by school board policy.

Your parents have been informed of the fight. We expect that you will apologize in person to the victim of your attack and that there will be no repetition of this kind of incident in the future.

This reprimand will become part of your record (student file) until the end of the school year If you are involved in any subsequent fighting incidents this year, appropriate disciplinary action will be taken, which may include suspension or expulsion.

If you have any questions about this reprimand or want to make a formal response, please contact the principal's office within ten school days.

Sincerely,

_____

*All formal letters of reprimand should be on school letterhead and hand-delivered, witnessed by a third party.

- Follow the six standard steps for reprimanding:
  1. State the offense or violation. Avoid rumor. Stick to facts.
  2. Explain the reason for the reprimand. Cite school policy if appropriate. No reprimand should come as a surprise.
  3. Allow time for explanation, rebuttal, questions, apology, or expressions of remorse. Be willing to change your mind if new information warrants it.
  4. Spell out expectations (what it will take to make things right), immediate penalties, and future consequences if the misbehavior reoccurs. Give choices if possible. Show students how they can make amends.
  5. Offer help and support if appropriate.
  6. Stop. That's all there is to it. Don't belabor the issue. Let life go on.
- Be prepared for negative reactions ranging from denial and protestations of innocence to belligerence and blasphemy. Teenagers particularly are hypersensitive to accusation, criticism, or reprimand. One of the changes of pubescence seems to be developing a very thin skin.

Some educators feel they should soften their reprimands to protect the student's psyche. They shouldn't. A reprimand is supposed to be bad news.

The right thing to say when giving a reprimand is simply to say what needs to be said and to say exactly what you mean. Anything less is an abdication of responsibility.

DEALING WITH TOUCHY TOPICS (ALCOHOL, DRUGS, SEX, EATING DISORDERS, AND OTHER AT-RISK BEHAVIORS)

It's hard to communicate with teens and younger students about sensitive at-risk behavior such as alcohol, sex, drugs, compulsive gambling, or eating disorders. Many parents can't or won't do it. That's why school leaders have to.

Avoiding touchy topics in schools is not an option. Kids today need conversations with adults about the risks and choices they face. The subject of sex is a good example.

Initiation of sexual activity keeps happening younger and younger because of earlier puberty and the influences of our sexually charged society. Worse yet, one-fourth of all new AIDS victims are teenagers. These alone are compelling reasons for school personnel to address the subject.

Unfortunately, even educators often have as much trouble as anyone else in finding just the right words to use or message to send. What do you say to kids about self-destructive behaviors? How do you say it? How do you get through to today's streetwise students? What does it take to be heard?

The answer is a combination of straight talk and "tough love." It starts by avoiding common communication mistakes, which can jeopardize your credibility and turn kids off.

It's easy not to be listened to or believed by young people when communicating about at-risk behaviors. There are lots of ways to short-circuit meaningful discussion or dialogue before it starts. Here's what most counselors agree you should not do when trying to interact with kids (verbally or in writing) about sex, drugs, or other compulsive, addictive, or destructive life choices:

- Don't start too late. The age of experimentation keeps dropping. It's never too early for school leaders to initiate age-appropriate dialogue about healthy living.
- Don't be dumb, naïve, or in denial about student behavior. Many of your students are engaging in at-risk conduct every day. Accept it. Don't talk or write as if no problem exists in your school(s). The kids know better.
- Don't walk on eggs or pussyfoot around tough subjects. Say what has to be said. That's what adults do. And it's your job.

- Don't perpetuate myths.
- Don't send mixed messages or perpetuate double standards.
- Don't be overly dramatic or resort to sensationalism. Avoid scare topics. Today's students don't scare easily.
- Don't scold. Students turn a deaf ear to lectures.
- Don't preach or moralize. Students know that many adults who preach abstinence experimented with at-risk behaviors themselves when they were young. Kids just figure it's their turn now.
- Don't talk pharmacology. You'll be out of your league and the kids will know it. They believe they can get more and better information from the Internet. They're probably right.
- Don't try to affect pseudo-street talk in an effort to be hip. You'll only appear ridiculous. Talk like a school leader. That's what students expect. That's what they'll listen to.
- Don't be argumentative or combative. If you engage in debate, you'll lose every time in the eyes of your students.
- Don't patronize, talk down to students, or belittle today's youth culture.
- Don't use psychobabble or act like a therapist. Your students know your limitations. You should too.
- Don't impose your values on kids; instead, urge them to discuss values with their families.
- Don't make promises you can't keep. (For instance, you can't honor promises of confidentiality if you hear about possible criminal activity.)

With all these pitfalls to avoid, what's left? What can edu-leaders say about dangerous habits and choices that will make a difference? How can they get important life-saving messages across? How can school leaders communicate effectively with students about alcohol, drugs, sex, eating disorders, and all other at-risk behaviors that threaten today's kids?

It's not easy, but it is possible if you are willing to speak up for what you know is right, to speak plainly and honestly about controversial topics, and to risk showing that you genuinely care.

The best administrators and teachers get through to kids about these sensitive subjects every day. You can too. Here's how the experts do it:

- Be sensitive to local mores. Saying things that will get you fired won't help you or your students very much.
- Communicate one-on-one or in small groups whenever possible. Talk, don't lecture; listen, don't yell; and inform, don't scare.
- Know what you are talking about. Stick to facts. Have your statistics straight. Don't guess, assume, or bluff. Students won't listen to baloney very long.
- Make sure your comments are age-appropriate. Don't give a college course to a six-year-old. If three sentences are enough, stop there.
- Remain calm. If you're too emotional, you'll scare off your audience.
- Be realistic. Don't downplay the power of addiction and compulsive behavior or expect miracles overnight.
- Make clear what you think and feel. Share your values. Show you give a damn. It's called teaching.
- Be careful about using street terms to communicate about at-risk activities and behaviors. The language of today's youth culture changes constantly. To communicate effectively, it is important that all educators remain current on youth jargon as it evolves over time. If you're not up-to-date, students won't listen to you, but they will laugh at you.
- Always treat nicotine and alcohol as gateway drugs. They shouldn't be dismissed lightly.
- Talk about why kids engage in at-risk behaviors (e.g., peer pressure, low self-esteem, experimentation, thrill seeking, gang influences, escape from pain or abuse,

negative role models, boredom, or just for fun). Point out alternatives.

- Communicate about consequences (physical and emotional) using real-world examples.
- Talk about solutions, possibilities, alternatives, and second chances.
- Acknowledge that sometimes there is a double standard in our society.
- Emphasize respect.
- Help kids learn that "no" means "no."
- Urge kids to listen to and dialogue with their parents.
- Talk about available help and how to get it.
- Talk about positive role models. Let boys know that there are heroes besides athletes and rock stars, and let girls see that not all successful women weigh less than 100 pounds.
- Talk about tools and coping skills such as self-affirmations, goal setting, reality checking, conflict resolution, social skills, meditation, relaxation techniques, treatment programs, and support groups.
- Answer questions with questions. Let students discover their own values, truths, and answers.
- Keep communicating. Don't back off or give up. Always keep the door open for further dialogue.

Sometimes, the best way to get through to students about sensitive subjects is to have someone else do it for you. If you can get kids talking to kids about responsible choices regarding sex, drugs, and other risky behaviors, the message may come through loud and clear. Students will often tolerate administrators and teachers, but they really listen to peers. That's why youth organizations such as SADD (Students Against Drunk Driving) are so successful.

Never be afraid to use the best available messenger. Whatever works is always the best way to communicate with students about emotional issues.

How to Talk to Kids About Death and Dying

Americans aren't very good at talking about death and dying. We'd rather ignore the whole subject. Sometimes, however, that is not an option for school leaders.

If someone close to one of your students dies or if the unexpected death of a teacher or classmate stuns the school, administrators and teachers have to deal with the issue. When students first experience personal loss through death, they are suddenly confronted with their own vulnerability and mortality. It's no surprise that they don't know how to react to death and have to look to adults for guidance and signals. In most situations, the buck stops at the schoolhouse door.

Death scares kids (as it does adults). Children between the ages of seven and nine are particularly prone to worry that others close to them might die and to wonder what will happen to them if other deaths do occur.

It is common for kids to express their fears and grief through behavior and play. Sometimes, they process their grief in intervals. Questions may pop up even months later. School personnel are better equipped to talk to students about death and dying if they understand these normal reactions.

In searching for ways to have meaningful dialogue with kids, a good beginning is to remind them that death is a natural part of living. All living things die, including plants, pets—and people.

The next step should be to provide needed reassurances, such as these:

- You are not going to die any time soon.
- You didn't do anything wrong. (Kids often wonder if they might have contributed to a death.)
- You will be taken care of.
- Grieving is OK.
- Adults will listen and help.

It also helps to encourage students to talk about their thoughts and feelings. Kids, like adults, usually process grief by experiencing seven distinct emotional phases:

1. Shock

2. Denial

3. Anger

4. Guilt

5. Sadness

6. Acceptance

7. Moving on

Giving young people permission to grieve, discussing the emotional phases of grief, and getting them to express their feelings can expedite the entire process.

Although there are no easy formulas for communicating with kids about death, help is available. The following additional advice from experienced grief counselors won't put words in your mouth, but will assist you to find the right thing to say in your own way:

- Sort out your own feelings about death before talking to your students about it.
- Don't dwell unduly on the sorrow, but don't forge ahead with business as usual, either. The issue must be adequately addressed so that all parties can move on.
- Don't hide behind platitudes or euphemisms. Avoid clichés. Shy away from such expressions as "passed away." Use the terms *die* and *death*. These are real words that convey a sense of finality and permanence. Kids need to get accustomed to hearing them. Don't try to talk like an undertaker. Talk like a regular person.
- Dare to display your own emotions. It's only natural. Disclosure of your feelings can help students validate their own.
- Don't rush to make some lesson out of the experience.

- Don't say anything to belittle student emotions.
- Be honest and factual.
- Use the right words to comfort and describe the emotions of loss (see Box 2.9).
- Don't over-eulogize. Don't make saints out of ordinary mortals. The students know what the deceased person was and was not without your help.
- Don't impose your own values and interpretations of death on your students.
- Don't try to explain "Why." You don't really know and your students know you don't know.
- Celebrate the life of the deceased.
- Talk about how to preserve the memories and honor the life of the deceased.
- Offer professional counseling for any students who need it.

Box 2.9   The Language of Grief and Healing

Belief	Loss	Sadness
Comfort	Love	Shock
Compassion	Martyr	Solace
Concern	Memorial	Sorrow
Condolences	Memories	Support
Consolation	Missed	Survivors
Disbelief	Pain	Sympathy
Emotions	Praise	Testimonial
Examples	Prayer	Tragic
Faith	Premature	Understanding
Healing	Recover	Unfortunate
Help	Remember	Untimely

In addition to the suggestions above, it is important to remember that, sometimes, the right thing to say is nothing. Educators can't always say some magic words to make things all right. They don't have to. Never be afraid of silence. It can allow time for students to express what they are wondering and experiencing. If your silence helps kids to label and affirm their feelings, that may be the greatest service you can offer.

HOW TO TALK TO TOUGH KIDS
(INCLUDING GANG MEMBERS)

School leaders are accustomed to communicating with different audiences, but many freeze up when it comes to dealing with the school's toughest kids—especially if they are gang members. It's not uncommon for even experienced professionals to feel uneasy, awkward, uncomfortable, and sometimes afraid when interacting with kids they know to be potentially violent and destructive.

Tough kids are scary—especially when they are gang members. They are a threat inside and outside of the school. Nevertheless, they are still students. They should be treated like all other students—firmly and fairly. Tough kids are still kids. They can be taught and untaught.

The right way to talk to students with hard-core behavior problems, including gang members, is the same way you talk to other students—calmly, directly, honestly, and face-to-face, without being baited or intimidated.

Other special tips for communicating with the school's toughest and most dangerous problem kids include the following:

- Be businesslike. And mean business.
- Strive to talk with the students, not at them.
- Control your emotions. Avoid yelling or screaming. It can easily be interpreted as a sign of weakness or panic. Speak firmly without raising your voice.
- Focus on problem solving. If possible, follow the four steps of traditional conflict resolution:
  1. Define the problem.
  2. Look for possible areas of agreement.
  3. Acknowledge what all parties are feeling.
  4. State your case as simply and clearly as possible.
- Remember, it's not written anywhere that there has to be a winner and a loser.
- Avoid arguing, pleading, contradicting, accusing, or saying anything to make the student unduly defensive.

- Don't bluff or make any threats or promises you can't keep.
- Avoid acts of false bravado, theatrics, or heroics. There's nowhere in your contract that says you have to be John Wayne.
- Don't rule out negotiating. It can work, even with gang members. (Even murderers plea-bargain.)
- Never agree to anything that weakens the school's position or makes a bad situation worse.
- Take all threats seriously.
- Continue the dialogue no matter what.
- Follow through. Keep your word. Do what you say you're going to do. This is absolutely essential to continued credibility.

It's one thing talking to tough kids. It's another thing if those tough kids happen to be gang members. The school has a message for gangs. Like it or not, as a school leader, you are the voice that has to make the message clear to all students, including the gang members themselves. The message is this:

- The school must be a safe haven for all kids.
- The school has a zero-tolerance, no-nonsense, no drugs, no guns, no violence policy. It will be enforced. Period.
- No gang regalia, insignias, signs, or graffiti are allowed on school property.
- The school and the community offer better and safer things to do and more ways to succeed and be recognized than any street gang.
- Support and help are available for students who want to get out of a gang.
- Gang members can find more positive leadership experiences in the school.

To get through to gang members, the first step is to acknowledge gang presence in your school. Denial only makes you look stupid or out of the loop.

Adults are more effective if they understand why gangs hold strong appeal for many at-risk students, even at the elementary level (see Box 2.10).

Box 2.10 Why Kids Join Gangs

Peer pressure	Identification
Money	Protection
Drugs	Boredom
Sex	Fear
Sense of belonging	Someplace to go when no one
(feeling of family)	else cares

The average age of new gang members is continually dropping. It's not uncommon for young children to be recruited to run errands for older gang members. Today's gangs are catch-alls for throwaway kids. These are the students you most need to talk to about gangs.

Gangs are only as strong as the community allows them to be. When schools are strong, gangs are weak. The right thing for school personnel to say to gang members, at any age, is that all kids are welcome; gangs are not.

How to Talk to Kids About School Violence

With or without gangs, schools are more violent than ever. It's a topic school personnel can't ignore. Whether it's a playground bully or a tragic school shooting, school leaders have to talk to kids about violence.

It's not a simple subject to discuss, but most psychologists agree that the following principles can make it easier for both parties to open up on the topic:

- Listen first to determine what students want and need to hear about threats of violence (i.e., reassurances, safety tips, etc.).
- Be honest, straightforward, and realistic, but avoid scare tactics.

- Stress that incidents of serious violence are rare, particularly in schools. Kids need to know that violence isn't inevitable.
- Reaffirm that most people still settle disputes or problems without violence.
- Be sure students know basic personal safety measures and precautions and where to go for added help when necessary.
- Use the opportunity to reteach lessons about tolerance, respect, civility, and peaceful conflict resolution techniques.

The worst thing educators can say about violence in schools is nothing. Scaring kids isn't your job. Preparing them for the real world is. When school leaders ignore unpleasant realities, the school itself becomes irrelevant. You can do better than that.

How to Talk to Kids About National Tragedies

Bad things happen and school leaders have to respond. The school can't buffer students from natural or man-made national tragedies (e.g., JFK assassination, 9/11, Columbine, hurricane Katrina, etc.). When the whole country is talking about a national disaster or catastrophic event, school leaders can't remain mute. Trying to insulate or isolate students from bad news doesn't help them grow and makes the school irrelevant to real life.

In times of national disaster, the role of school leaders and other personnel is to help students understand, assimilate, and process what happened without becoming unduly frightened or traumatized. The following guidelines can help:

- Explain to students what is *known* about the event, not what is speculated. Don't overanalyze or provide too much interpretation. Stick to the facts.
- Use language the pupils understand. Avoid too many technical or scientific terms.

- Present information calmly and factually.
- Don't downplay, minimize, or trivialize the event—but don't sensationalize it either.
- Don't overload kids with graphic images that can become the stuff of nightmares. (There's a reason why many schools turned off all TV monitors on 9/11.)
- Be reassuring.
- Share your own honest feelings and emotions, including confusion and sadness. Let students know it's OK to be scared or to cry.
- If possible, used the moment to teach something worthwhile about preparedness, helpfulness, compassion, and human resiliency. If appropriate, channel student energy toward thinking of ways they can memorialize, honor, or help the victims.
- Arrange for counselors to assist students in dealing with their individual grief or fears as needed.

The important thing to remember in communicating with children and teens about tragedies is that your behavior (how you act, what you say, and how you say it) serves as a model, teaching them how to handle disasters and catastrophic events in their own lives. This is when they need a grown-up. That's why you are there.

Following the advice offered throughout this chapter can make it possible for you to communicate effectively with all students in any school situation. It's as good as guaranteed.

Not all educators can be brilliant or charismatic, but they all can communicate clearly and honestly with candor, patience, and respect. No student can expect more. No real school leader can do less.

It all boils down to using straight talk and common sense when speaking or writing to kids. That's how the very best school leaders get through to their students. It will get through to your students as well. Try it. It works every time.

3

How to Say the Right Thing to Parents

Some educators are more comfortable talking to kids than to adults. Nevertheless, effective communication with parents is part of the bargain for all school leaders. It's not just nice to be able to say the right thing to parents in all situations. It's absolutely essential! Parents are the bread and butter of the school.

No school can work unless the home-school partnership works. Period. As a school leader, you need parents as much as they need you.

Anyone can alienate parents. A course in how to chase off parents would only take about two minutes. Unfortunately, however, it's not always that easy to get through to all parents and to gain and galvanize their support. But that's what school leaders do. That's what school leaders have to do. It starts by removing barriers.

WHAT TO SAY TO PUT PARENTS AT EASE

Whether you are dealing with one parent, a roomful, or an audience of thousands, there are always communication obstacles that have to be overcome.

Parents often bring barriers and baggage to the table. Some have a history of bad experiences with school authorities. Others distrust school officials because they think the school discriminates against them and their children. Still others are simply uncomfortable with all institutions and authority figures. The fancier your title, the more uneasy many parents will be. All of these feelings hamper communication.

Likewise, educators themselves frequently create communication roadblocks by being vague, noncommittal, arrogant, or patronizing, giving way too much or too little information, using too much jargon, or adopting a Pollyannaish attitude.

It's your job to find ways to lower these barriers. It's up to you, as a leader of the school, to find the right words to put parents at ease and win them over to your point of view.

Communication is easier if you remember that there is not just one single parent audience. There are many parent publics, including:

- Working parents
- Single parents
- Adoptive parents
- Minority parents
- College-educated parents
- High school parents
- Immigrant parents
- Teen parents
- Gay parents
- Unmarried parents
- Biracial parents
- Welfare parents

Sending clear messages will always be more effective if you target the potential audience you're trying to reach. The words you use—even the language you use—and how you use them will vary depending on the target audience.

Regardless of their background, parents will be comfortable with your message only if they accept you as believable. Credibility begins and ends with telling the truth. Whenever you don't know what to say to parents, try honesty. It works.

Although there are no secret formulas for putting parents at ease and making them more receptive to your viewpoint, there are a few tricks of the trade commonly used by successful school leaders everywhere:

- Project self-assurance. Act like you know what you're doing. (Who knows? Maybe you do.) The more confidence you have, the more confidence the audience will have in what you say.
- If possible, when dealing with a single set of parents, make it clear right away that you know about their children and the issue at hand. When communicating with a group of parents, make it plain that you understand the situation and the concerns involved. Show that you've done your homework.
- Be friendly. Smile. Make eye contact. If meeting with a small group, offer your handshake first. Repeat the parents' names. Remember them. If others are present, make introductions all around to put everyone at ease. Sometimes, part of saying the right thing is doing all the right things first to pave the way for what's said later.
- Talk in ordinary words. It's more important to be understood than to sound well educated. (If this sounds familiar, you're catching on.)
- Demonstrate empathy. Bill Clinton had it right when he repeatedly declared, "I feel your pain." Audiences buy what you say if they think you care.
- Respect the parent's point of view if it differs from your own. After all, even school leaders don't have a monopoly on the truth.

- Practice self-disclosure. Make "no secrets, no surprises" your mantra when dealing with parents.
- Avoid technical educationese, big words, buzzwords, clichés, pompous language, and patronizing or arrogant statements.
- Listen more than you talk. Practice active listening.
- Use unifying terms such as *we, teamwork, partnership,* and *together.*
- Avoid appearing manipulative. Like everyone else, parents hate to feel used.
- Tell parents up front what you want or need.
- Admit mistakes. Be willing to say, "I don't know" instead of offering lame excuses.
- Give parents all the time they need to feel they have been heard.
- Pledge your best efforts to respond to parents' concerns. Mean it. Do it.

It's pretty hard not to be understood and accepted when you use the communication tools and techniques above.

There are also a few special pointers that can further help you get directions and instructions across to parents when it's absolutely necessary that they follow them.

SUCCESS SECRETS FOR COMMUNICATING "MUST-KNOW" INFORMATION

Let's face it. The school has more to say than most parents want to hear. Every week, administrators and teachers send tons of information home with students that never gets read. From the parents' perspective, the school generates as much junk mail as anyone else. Ouch!

So what can you do with important directions or instructions that are absolutely, positively necessary for parents to get, understand, and follow? The answer is to launch a full-scale communication blitz.

When conveying "must-know" information to parents, effective school leaders pull out all the stops and resort to the fine art of "deliberate repetition." This is a case where how *often* you say it is as important as what you say or how you say it. It doesn't matter if you say the right thing if no one hears or reads it.

No matter how critical your message is, never assume that every parent reads it the first time, understands it, or cares about it. Likewise, don't rely completely on others to pass on essential information secondhand.

The trick is to hammer home your point using every available means of communication:

- Send announcements home with elementary students. Secondary school students aren't always reli able couriers. It may pay to alert the kids that this message is different and shouldn't be lost in the bot tom of an overstuffed backpack.
- Include it in the school or district newsletter.
- If it's important enough, mail a personal letter to every parent. That's what bulk mail rates are for.
- Put the information on the district, school, or classroom Web site.
- Record the information on your voice mail message and/or the school hotline.
- Ask the local media to include the instructions in newscasts or public service announcements.
- Write a letter to the editor, if appropriate.
- Send e-mail messages to all parents linked to the Internet.
- When all else fails, use a telephone tree to personally contact each family directly.
- Repeat as necessary.

Obviously, this kind of blitz has to be used sparingly or it will lose its impact. Save it for the really big stuff. (Remember the story of the boy who cried wolf too many times.)

Other tips that can help ensure that your top-priority instructions get across to parents include the following:

- Pare your message down to bare-bones simplicity. Use key words and short phrases. Limit the amount of text.
- Use bold print for key facts.
- Remember, Americans are a visual people. Use illustrations, charts, diagrams, or maps where appropriate.
- Mark the announcement "URGENT."
- Put really crucial information on different-colored paper.
- Be complete. Be sure you have included all necessary details (i.e., deadlines, dates, time, locations, materials needed, costs, etc.).
- If you want action, ask for it. Be specific.
- Don't send out critical information too far in advance. It's not just kids who have short attention spans any more.
- If your instructions include deadlines, stick to them. Once you start waffling on deadlines, parents will quit paying attention to them.

The bottom line is that the key to getting must-know information to parents is to

- Say it accurately.
- Say it completely.
- Say it clearly.
- Say it in many different ways.
- Say it often.

If all this effort seems like a lot of work, it is. As it turns out, giving simple instructions isn't so simple after all. Don't make the mistake of thinking it is.

STRAIGHT TALK AT PARENT-TEACHER CONFERENCES

The only thing wrong with parent conferences is that they are largely a matter of preaching to the choir. The parents whom the school most desperately needs to contact usually don't show up.

Nevertheless, the traditional parent-teacher conference is still the single best venue for direct contact with parents on a one-to-one basis. It's too good an opportunity to miss out on. This may be the best chance you will ever have to get all the right things said. Don't blow it.

The first step is to get as many parents as possible—even the hard-to-reach ones—to attend. Try serving food, providing child care, offering valet parking, and giving away door prizes. Whatever works. Shoot for 100% attendance. Celebrate if you get 70% or more. Work harder if you get only 50% or less participation.

Many schools put out a list of suggestions to help parents make the most of their conferences. This assumes that the educators involved already know all the right things to do. That's not always the case. Here are some standard guidelines that school personnel (administrators and teachers) should follow to wring maximum benefit from each parent-teacher conference:

- Have a specific goal in mind for every conference. If you don't know what you hope or expect to accomplish, you will never know if you are successful.
- Make it clear right away that you know which child is theirs. The greatest turnoff for parents is to sense that the teacher or administrator doesn't really know their child as an individual.
- Listen. Welcome parental questions and input. After all, parents know things about their child that school personnel don't. Always ask parents directly what they want the school to know about their child.

- Tell parents what they need to hear, not just what they want to hear. Find the simplest way to say it. Dust off all your straight-talk skills. It may be now or never.
- Deal with more than letter grades and numbers. Report cards (progress reports) can do that. Talk about feelings, impressions, attitudes, and values.
- If there is a problem, get it out on the table. Be sensitive, but be scrupulously honest. Provide details and examples. Don't blame the parents for the problem. Get their input. Get their ideas. Get their help. And get on with solving the situation.
- Try to avoid an adversarial (you/us) atmosphere. Stress cooperation and partnership.
- Give the parents as accurate a picture of their child's development as possible. Use examples or a portfolio of the student's work and make meaningful comparisons. The best comparison is with the child's own potential. Downplay comparisons with siblings, friends, or other classmates.
- Be as upbeat and encouraging as appropriate. No conference should be all negative. Say something good about every child. (Yes, there is something good to say about even the worst kid in school.) Use positive words as much as possible (see Box 3.1). All parents need to know their kid is going to make it.
- Emphasize choices and opportunities.
- Give all parents their full allotment of time. Begin and end on time. If necessary, be accessible or follow up and make arrangements to meet again soon.
- Ask parents what they want to volunteer for. Don't ask if they want to volunteer. It's too easy to say "no." If you can actually get parents actively involved, you will have gone a long way toward gaining their acceptance and support.

Box 3.1   Encouraging Words for Parent-Teacher Conferences

Ability	Desire	Progress
Accomplishment	Effort	Results
Achievement	Gains	Rewards
Admire	Goals	Satisfactory
Appreciation	Good	Scores
Benefit	Growth	Solutions
Best	Performance	Success
Better	Positive	Support
Constructive	Potential	Understanding
Cooperation	Practice	Work
Creativity	Pride	
Credit	Proactive	

- Thank parents for their efforts. Let them know you understand that parenting is a tough job at best.
- Always end with an agreed-upon action plan.

There is no better time to communicate with parents than conference time. It is an opportunity, not an obligation. If you don't say the right things to parents here, they may never be said. And that will be your fault.

How to Explain Grades and Test Scores

Letter grades and standardized test scores are valuable tools for communicating with parents. They can also be confusing and misleading if misinterpreted. They need to be carefully explained to be useful. Guess who gets to do the explaining. It's up to school leaders to clarify for parents what grades and test scores are and are not. The "nots" may be the most important.

No single test score can tell anyone very much about a child. They are not valid or reliable enough for that. Someone needs to tell parents about this. If you don't, who will?

Likewise, grades are important indices and records of performance. But they are not flawless, and they are not very scientific. No administrator or teacher should pretend to parents that they are.

Too many parents put too much stock in grades and test results. That's largely the school's fault. These parents think test results and letter grades are better measures than they really are. Some even believe that a single grade or score can be used as the basis for making significant life choices. That's scary.

As a professional educator, what you say to parents about grades and test scores is important. The guidelines below can help you get it right:

Tips for Talking to Parents About Standardized Test Scores

- Know what you're talking about before trying to explain test results to parents. If you're uncomfortable clarifying the difference between percentages and percentiles, don't even try. Get help or let someone else do it.
- Put parents at ease by assuring them that the results are understandable. Many parents are intimidated by test scores.
- Be sure that parents understand what the test is designed to measure (i.e., general knowledge, ability, achievement, etc.).
- Explain that all tests have built-in flaws.
- Help parents understand that no child can or should be defined by a single score.
- Describe how the test is normed. Parents want to know with what population their child is being compared.
- Explain how the test results are to be used. The answer should be to drive instruction, not label kids.
- Explain how the test result is reported (e.g., percentile, grade equivalent, etc.).
- Don't baffle parents with statistical or psychometric mumbo jumbo (e.g., standard deviation, standard error of measurement, etc.). Most parents don't want to know all that stuff. They just want to learn how their child did.
- Explain as carefully, clearly, and simply as you can what the child's score really means. For example, don't just say the score is at the 70th percentile. Define percentile rank. Clarify that it doesn't mean the student

got 70% of the answers correct, but that the child scored as well as or better than 70% of the kids taking the test.
- Answer all questions. Keep at it until both you and the parents are convinced they understand the score and what it means. Otherwise the whole conversation has merely been an exercise in futility.
- Be sure parents understand the many extraneous factors that can influence a given score, such as student fatigue, a headache, or outside distractions.
- End by eliciting parental help in convincing kids to take all standardized tests seriously (similar to the message in the sample letter in Box 3.2).

Box 3.2 Sample Parent Letter on Testing

Dear Parents:

On January 10–12, all sixth-grade pupils will be taking the State Graduation Basic Skills Tests in reading, writing, math, science, and social studies. All students must score at least 65% correct answers on each of these tests in order to graduate from high school. (It's the law.)

Students who do not achieve the graduation standard in sixth grade will be referred for summer schooling or tutoring and will have other opportunities to take the tests in the eighth and/or twelfth grades.

Many students at this level do not take standardized tests seriously. Please help us impress upon your child their importance. This is the time for every student to do his or her best. You can also help by giving your child a pep talk before the test date and see to it that your child eats properly and gets plenty of rest during the testing period.

Your child's graduation standard test results will be reported and interpreted for you before the end of the school year. Thank you for your cooperation. If you have any further questions, please call the Principal's office at _____.

Sincerely,

_____

Parents may pay attention to standardized test scores, but they are much more obsessed with grades. Letter grades as recorded in periodic pupil progress reports (report cards) are among the most personal communications between the school and the home. That's why report cards are easily the most avidly read documents the school produces.

Parents believe that grades are meaningful. But this is true only if they really understand what their child's grades represent. That can take some tall explaining, as indicated below.

Tips for Talking to Parents About Grades and Report Cards

- Start by explaining that grades are useful only if they reflect what the school purports to teach.
- Be sure parents understand that all letter grades are somewhat arbitrary. No matter how many mathematical calculations and formulas are involved in determining a given grade, it ends up being a subjective teacher judgment call. In the final analysis, grades are one person's documented opinion or assessment of another person's performance. No more. No less. It's easy for school officials to say that 70% is passing, but it must be remembered that they picked the 70% standard and they decided 70% of what. Someone else might do it differently. No two teachers grade exactly alike. This is must-know information for parents. If you don't make this point clear, you're doing a disservice to parents.
- Be thorough in explaining your personal grading system—how you arrive at individual student grades. What counts? What doesn't? What about extra credit? Do you use pluses and minuses? Why or why not? If so, how do you split hairs to determine who gets the plus and minus marks? If you can't make your grading process readily understandable to parents, you're doing something wrong. It shouldn't take a CPA to decipher any school's grading system.

- Once you've explained the system, pinpoint exactly how and why the child got a specific grade—what the child did and didn't do to earn the mark.
- Always supplement the letter grade with supporting comments either on the report card or verbally (see Box 3.3). No grade should stand alone without clarification and backup data.
- End by explaining what it will take for the student to change or improve the grade. Be specific. Answer all questions.

Box 3.3   Sample Supporting Comments for Report Cards

Actively participates	Uses time efficiently
Follows directions	Works independently
Applies skills	Inattentive
Displays self-control	Needs better organization
Shows initiative (self-starter)	Insufficient effort
Has a positive attitude	Turns in sloppy work
Exhibits leadership work	Missing or incomplete work
Takes pride in work	

Coming up with test scores and letter grades is easy. Explaining them isn't. Don't take the task lightly. How you break any good or bad news makes a difference.

HOW TO SHARE GOOD NEWS WITH PARENTS

It's not every day that parents get good news from the school. When it happens, it should be done right. Whether it's awarding a college scholarship to a deserving student or announcing that the entire school has been recognized by the federal government as a National School of Excellence, good news is currency that should be spent carefully to maximize the glow. It's too good an opportunity to pass up.

Schools take a lot of bashing from politicians, the media, and society in general. When something good happens, it pays to blow the school's horn a little.

Obviously, breaking good news isn't rocket science or brain surgery. Anyone can do it. But the most successful school leaders know how to multiply its impact by following a few commonsense do's and don'ts:

Do's
- Let the parents, students, or staff members involved be the first to know before going public.
- Be clear and specific about the nature of the good news and what it means to the school and the parties involved.
- Give full public credit (and maybe a little more) to all those who contributed to the success.
- Allow the parties involved to enjoy the moment. Get out of their way for a while.
- Let people know about it. Humility can take a backseat for a while. Make the most of the opportunity to remind people of other triumphs and to portray the school as a place where good things happen.
- Be reasonably brief. Don't belabor the point. Savor the success and move on.
- Act excited and happy about the good news. Enthusiasm is contagious.

Don'ts
- Don't tease people or try to be coy. Get to the point.
- Don't gild the lily. Don't blow the occasion out of proportion or make the triumph seem like more than it really is.
- Don't get carried away with superlatives. People will think it's the first time anything good ever happened to the school.
- Don't try to act cool or stifle your emotions. Feelings are allowed.
- Don't take undue credit for what happened.
- Don't qualify the good news. Save the caveats and allow people to enjoy the triumph for what it is.

- Don't use the situation to add more pressure to those involved (e.g., "Now you can do even better by _____.").

The most important point is not to let good news go unnoticed. When good people do a good job, they deserve to feel good about it. You can make it happen by what you say and how you say it.

How to Break Bad News (Failure, Retention, Disciplinary Action, Athletic Ineligibility)

Students screw up, make mistakes, fail courses, skip school, use drugs, get into fights, have accidents, break bones, break laws, and get into every conceivable kind of trouble. Bad news happens in school every day. When it does, it's a lot harder to talk to parents about than good news and not nearly as much fun.

Communicating with parents about infractions, penalties, or other bad news regarding their child is always painful. But the worst thing school leaders can do about breaking bad news is not to do it. Sitting on bad news, glossing over it, or denying it altogether won't work. Getting it out on the table will. It's the old straight-talk thing again. It's always difficult to find the right words to break bad news to parents, but it's a lot easier if you consider the following additional pointers:

- Timing is everything. The rule of thumb is that the best time to break bad news is at the earliest possible opportunity. Bad news only gets worse if left unattended. Try to find a time when parents will be most ready and able to receive, accept, and cope with negative information.
- Don't play mind games (e.g., trying to soften bad news by linking it with some offsetting good news). Such ploys are transparent and seldom work. Bad news is supposed to be bad (unpleasant). Diluting it won't make it any better. Real adults can handle harsh

realities. Hopefully, you and the parents involved will fall into that category.

- Tell it like it is. Refuse to be vague. Make sure you are perfectly clear about what is going on and why. Talk to parents about:
  1. What was
  2. What is
  3. What has to be (consequences)
  4. What's possible (alternatives and options)
  5. What's likely
  6. What's preferred
- Cover everything the parents may need to know about the situation, including student rights, time frames, choices available, pending legal action, hearing opportunities, grievance procedures, referral possibilities, and where to go for help.
- Don't search for the safest, softest words or the kindest words. Look for the right words. The simplest, clearest, most precise, and accurate ones.
- Be certain, not tentative.
- Be courteous, but restrained. Your demeanor speaks volumes about the seriousness of the situation.
- Don't personalize the episode. It's about bad news, not about a bad kid or bad parents.
- Deal with emotions. Bad news evokes strong feelings. Let the parents vent to get their emotions out in the open.
- Commit to appropriate follow-up.
- End with hope. (There always is some, no matter how bad the news is.)

You can't turn bad news into good news. But you can turn bad news around. It starts by using the advice above to help you say the right thing in the right way. If the bad news deals with serious student misbehavior that the parents must know about, there are a few other tips you should know.

DON'T BEAT AROUND THE BUSH
ABOUT BAD BEHAVIOR

If breaking bad news to parents is the pits, breaking bad news about their child's bad behavior is an even deeper black hole. Bad news about student misbehavior is hard to give and harder to receive. But it is a necessary building block in the home-school partnership. Problems can't get better until people talk about them.

You can never predict how parents will react to charges against their child. They may be angry or anxious, cooperative or combative, defensive or devastated, or simply in denial. This makes getting across to them a delicate process. Obviously, this is one of those sticky, tricky communication problems they don't teach you how to handle in graduate school. You'll see it here first.

If you think there is a viable alternative to straight talk, you have never had to tell parents that their child is in serious trouble with the school, the law, or both. This is a task that takes attention-grabbing, hit-'em-between-the-eyes plain speech and a no-frills delivery.

The rock-bottom rule for talking to parents about serious behavior problems is to be absolutely straightforward and to tell the unadorned truth in simple language. No hedging. There is no innocuous, gentle way to say, "Your kid is a thief," or "a drug dealer," or "a sex offender." So just do it. Don't hide behind euphemisms or metaphors. Use real words for real behaviors (see Box 3.4) because this is one message that has to get across to parents.

It's easier to communicate with parents about pupil misconduct if you adopt a "no-fault attitude." What you want is parental cooperation, not guilt. Stay away from unsubstantiated allegations, finger-pointing, blaming, shaming, or name-calling. Omit any references to rumor or hearsay. Likewise, avoid moralizing or passing judgment. Stick to facts.

Box 3.4   Vocabulary for Breaking Bad News About
            Pupil Misbehavior

Abuse	Drive-by	Prostitution
Accessory	Drug use	Rape
Addict	Extortion	Reckless driving
Arrested	Fake ID	Repeat offender
Arson	Felony	Resisting arrest
Assault	Fence	Robbery
Battery	Gambling	Runaway
Betting	Gang activity	Sexual assault
Binge	Gang bang	Sexual harassment
Bomb threat	Graffiti	Sexual misconduct
Breaking and entering	Hacking	Shoplifting
Bribe	Hate crime	Smoking
Bullying	Hazing	Soliciting
Burglary	Hit and run	Stalking
Carjacking	Indecent exposure	Statutory rape
Cheating	Insubordination	Stealing
Chop shop	Interrogated	Subpoena
Computer virus	Intoxicated	Swastikas
Concealed weapon	Legal limit	Tardiness
Confession	Lineup	Terroristic threats
Con game	Lying	Trespassing
Conspiracy	Misdemeanor	Truancy
Contraband	Molestation	Undercover
Controlled substance	Neo-Nazi	Vandalism
Corruption	Perjury	Vice
Counterfeiting	Pimp	Victim
(aggravated forgery)	Plagiarism	Violation
Cover-up	Plaintiff	Violence
Dealing	Plea bargain	Window peeping
Delinquency	Possession	Zero tolerance
Disorderly conduct	Profanity	
Disrespectful	Property damage	

The idea is to focus on behavior, not personalities. Be objective and businesslike. Don't play judge and jury. You're not a prosecutor; you're a representative of the school trying to enforce rules and help at-risk kids get back on track.

No more. No less. Last, don't even think about offering legal advice. If you want to be a lawyer, go to law school.

With these cautions and caveats in mind, the steps below can increase the odds of getting through to parents and arriving at a positive resolution or outcome:

- Follow all the advice on breaking bad news in the preceding section.
- Back up what you say with substantive proof or evidence (e.g., eyewitnesses, confession, videotape).
- Inform parents of the precise rule, policy, or law the child has violated. Give them a copy if appropriate.
- Make it clear what consequences the student faces. Don't negotiate or plea-bargain. That's somebody else's job.
- Try not to alienate the parents. Don't exhibit signs of anger, bias, or hostility. Keep in mind that you will have to deal with these people again in the future.
- Record or document everything said in the conference. It's usually wise to have a third-party witness on hand as well.
- The more serious the offense, the more legalistic your language may have to become. Don't hesitate to contact the school's legal counsel if needed.
- Inform the parents of any existing grievance or appeal process.
- If resolution is reached, it is often a nice touch to end up by offering the parents some help or advice on how to keep their child out of trouble in the future (see sample Parent Tip Sheet in Box 3.5).
- Be prepared to conduct all necessary follow-up.
- If a face-to-face conference can't be arranged or doesn't work out as planned, put all of the information above in writing (see Box 3.6 for a sample letter). Be sure to be as clear and forthright on paper as you would be in person.

Box 3.5   Parent Tip Sheet

How to Help Your Child Stay Out of Trouble at School
- Monitor your child's friendships. Peer pressure is good if your child has the right peers.
- Network with other parents. Work together to keep track of what your kids are doing.
- Watch your own behavior. Kids react more to how you live your life than to how you tell them to live theirs.
- Talk together as a family—every day.
- Talk openly about the values you live by.
- Establish and enforce a curfew.
- Stick to a regular bedtime.
- Limit TV and computer time.
- Celebrate successes (great or small) at school.
- Model patience and sticking to a task.
- Show interest in your child's school life (even in high school).
- Help your child get involved in afterschool activities.
- Spend time in your child's classroom if possible.
- Talk to your child's teachers—not just at conference time, but whenever needed.
- Keep track of your child's homework assignments.
- Model goal setting.
- Show your child how mature people solve disputes without violence.
- Keep guns under tight security.
- Support positive youth organizations such as SADD (Students Against Drunk Driving).

Even if you do everything by the numbers, there will be occasions when efforts to break bad news to parents about their child's misbehavior won't work the first time. Some parents won't listen, won't hear, won't believe, and won't cooperate. What do you do then?

Keep trying. Persistence is a lifestyle for effective school leaders. If you're tempted not to try again, just think what will happen to the student if you don't.

Box 3.6   *Sample Letter About Student Misbehavior*

Dear Parent:

Starting tomorrow, January 15, your child, Joe, is excluded from riding the regular school bus to and from school. As indicated in previous communications, Joe has been a chronic troublemaker on the bus since the first day of school. He has consistently violated bus safety rules by leaving his seat, bothering other students, throwing things, and showing disrespect to the driver. Even though I have talked to Joe about this unacceptable behavior on three separate occasions and assigned him to detention for three days, his conduct has not improved.

This morning, Joe shoved another child to the floor and started scuffling while the bus was in motion. This most recent incident has caused me to write this letter.

For obvious safety reasons, Joe must learn to follow bus rules in order to ride the bus. Free bus transportation is a privilege, not an entitlement.

Joe may not resume riding the bus until we have met to work out a plan to ensure Joe's compliance with established rules. You will be responsible for transporting him to and from school in the meantime.

Please contact my office to schedule a meeting as soon as possible. If I do not hear from you, my secretary will contact you to make an appointment.

If we work together, I'm sure we can resolve this serious matter.

Sincerely,

_____

Principal

How to Talk to Parents About Student Secrets, Surprises, and Other Sensitive Subjects (Dependency, Pregnancy, Homosexuality)

Kids are full of surprises. Many also have deep, dark secrets they don't want anyone (especially their parents) to know about. Many of these sensitive confidences involve hush-hush topics that would easily cause embarrassment or trauma to their entire family if revealed.

Many of these carefully kept secrets are not primarily the school's business. They should be largely personal and private family matters, such as substance abuse, pregnancy, sexually transmitted disease, or gay or lesbian lifestyles. These are secrets or surprises that someone else—preferably the students involved—should divulge to parents. Unfortunately, it doesn't always work out that way.

Sometimes, circumstances dictate that school leaders must be the bearers of sensitive revelations to parents. If it happens to you, you have absolutely nothing to fall back on except complete frankness, honest dialogue, and a compassionate heart. Here are the twelve steps to take to make sure such an exchange is as professional, productive, painless, and helpful as possible:

1. Ensure a private setting and leave instructions for no interruptions.

2. Set the tone immediately. Come across as concerned and serious from the very start. Don't begin with an upbeat, business-as-usual greeting and then switch to a "by the way, a terrible thing has happened" mode.

3. Get the parents' full attention before revealing the reason for the conference.

4. Get to the point quickly. Say what has to be said without lengthy preliminaries. Use language that is clear, truthful, and professional. Avoid mistakenly using any offensive terms such as "knocked up" or "homo." Intentionally speak slowly to ensure understanding.

5. Repeat the information. You don't want any of the facts or details to pass over the parents' heads.

6. Check for reactions and understanding. Be absolutely sure that the parents grasp your full meaning.

7. Expect shock, anger, disbelief, denial, resistance, even combativeness. Don't take it personally. After all, how would you react if you were hearing this kind of information about your child?

8. Pause. Allow an incubation period. Parents may need a few moments of silence to let it all sink in. This may be the time to pull out the Kleenex.

9. Answer all questions and offer help, including counseling and referral.

10. Urge the parents to talk to their child as soon as possible. This is the next critical step.

11. Pledge your confidentiality, but indicate that continued secrecy is unlikely.

12. Agree to meet again later, if necessary, after the parents have had time to assimilate all you have told them.

When revealing sensitive secrets, one key to maintaining composure and controlling emotions is to concentrate more on how the parents are feeling and less on your own reactions. Sometimes, you have to get out of yourself in order to relate effectively to others. This same psychology works when communicating (or trying to) with parents who are mad as hell, off the wall, and out of control.

What to Say to Angry, Out-of-Control Parents and Other Adults

People—including parents and taxpayers—are getting crazier all the time. Anger seems to have become the national emotion.

Unfortunately, schools are no longer immune from the volatile (and sometimes violent) emotional outbursts that increasingly characterize our society.

We've all heard of "road rage" and "workplace rage." Now meet "school rage." From angry shouting matches at school board meetings and mobs of protestors storming the principal's office to irate parents showing up at the classroom door, school leaders are dealing with more angry, out-of-control people than ever before. And it's not going to get any better very soon.

Nobody likes it, but it's part of doing business as a school leader today. If you can't stand the heat, don't just stay out of the kitchen—get out of the entire building. For the faint of heart, this may be the time to change professions. For all the rest of us, it may be easy to feel helpless when confronted with chaotic parental behavior, but it's not necessary. There are still lots of ways for rational people to handle irrational people. Read on.

The simplest advice is that the right thing to say to angry people is the same thing you would say if they weren't angry: the truth. But there's more to it than that.

Whether communicating with an enraged crowd or a single angry individual, the first consideration is not to do anything to make matters worse. There are plenty of ways to pour fuel on the fire by saying or doing something that only makes angry people angrier.

For example, Jesse Ventura, who thrives on controversy, has been known to wear a T-shirt that says

Admit nothing.
Deny everything.
Counterattack.

This is not a conciliatory approach. It may work for ex-wrestlers, but it's not recommended for school officials trying to get across to disgruntled parents. Other common inflammatory acts to avoid when interacting with riled-up parents are shown in the list of "don'ts" in Box 3.7.

Box 3.7   Don'ts for Dealing With Out-of-Control People

---

1. Don't hide behind a pit-bull secretary or assistant. The best way to respond to attacks is to meet them head-on and try to resolve the issue face-to-face.
2. Don't belittle, downplay, ignore, or deny whatever is bothering or angering people. If they think it is a problem, it is a problem.
3. Don't overreact.
4. Don't try to bully or intimidate angry parents.
5. Don't immediately get defensive. Hear the complainants out.
6. Don't contradict or try to change the subject.
7. Don't take the bait and allow yourself to get caught up in a debate or a shouting match.
8. Don't babble or whine.
9. Don't resort to abusive language, phony excuses, double talk, or scapegoating.
10. Don't say too much. You might just stir things up more.
11. Don't offer token remedies.
12. Don't issue ultimatums, say never, or make promises you can't keep.

Saying the right thing while under pressure or attack requires self-control. ("Managing a difficult person means first managing yourself." —Carol Tavris) The more you can keep your emotions in check, the more likely you are to find the right words to fit the occasion. One cool head is worth a dozen hot heads.

Remember, if you allow angry people to make you angry, you've joined the crowd and forfeited your clear thinking and objectivity in the process. Once you "lose it," you won't get it back easily.

Often, the wisest thing to say initially to an angry individual or group is nothing. Hear them out first. Sometimes, people who have lost control only want to vent and be heard. They really don't expect anything specific. Listening can defuse the rage.

Consequently, don't even think about saying anything until you've tried to find out what's really bothering these people. Listen. Ask questions for clarification. Probe. Rephrase what you think you have heard to check for understanding. Get all the facts.

Once you fully understand what triggered this eruption or confrontation, it may be possible to take words out of their mouths by proposing the very course of action they have in mind or, better yet, a more beneficial remedy they haven't even thought of. This is one way to leapfrog from goat to hero in a single bound. That's leadership!

Other things to think about when communicating with angry, unruly individuals or groups include the following:

- If possible, gather information about the upset parents in advance of the face-to-face meeting. The better prepared you are, the better the session will go.
- Do what you can to establish rapport with the angry parties.
- Set boundaries for the discussion, including a time limit.
- Look on the dialogue as an opportunity rather than a threat.
- Depersonalize the situation. Angry patrons obviously want something, but it's probably not you.
- Try to shift the emphasis from confrontation to mutual problem solving.
- Respond in a calming manner (speak with a smile). Control the level, pitch, and volume of your voice. Give "soft" answers. A quiet voice and a friendly face can go a long way to reducing tension. Slow motions also have a quieting effect. Calm can be contagious. Often, an unruly crowd will eventually begin to mirror your professional, relaxed demeanor.
- Remain civil no matter what happens.
- Always attack problems, not people.
- Keep an open mind. Even an out-of-control mob just might be right.
- Give honest answers and support good suggestions made by the parents.

- If things get tense, use the "power of the pause" to reduce the level of intensity. Stop. Wait. Let others quiet down. Then proceed.
- If appropriate, use levity to help people lighten up, but use sparingly. Humor can backfire.
- If necessary, call in your "chits." Some of these people owe you something more than trouble.
- Apologize if necessary.
- Refuse to make any final decisions or long-term commitments in an emotionally charged atmosphere. It's OK to pledge to study, consider, look into the matter, and/or make a good-faith effort to resolve the problem. Nothing more.
- Sometimes, the best you can do is to respectfully agree to disagree without being disagreeable. This is best done by remaining pleasant, avoiding loaded language, and looking for areas of agreement.
- If possible, bring closure to the meeting by summarizing and setting a future date to report back and resume the discussion.
- Know when to walk away. If things are so out of control that progress is impossible, shut down. Turn off the mike. Turn off the light. Lock up. Leave.
- Always have predetermined plans for safety and security. When emotions are high, there is always some risk. Be ready for it.

School officials are often tempted to write off or ignore unreasonable or out-of-control parents and community members. But that doesn't make them go away.

As a community leader, it's your obligation to communicate with parents, patrons, and the public when they are angry and upset, as well as when they are happy and contented. The trick is to be consistent and be professional in both situations. It also helps to remember that no situation is irrevocably out of control as long as you remain in control.

MORE POINTERS FOR SAYING THE RIGHT THING TO PARENTS

When you are ready for more, there is always more to learn. Below are a few final pointers that may be just what you're looking for the next time you're stuck for what to say to parents:

- Parents are more receptive to what you have to say if they believe you are available to them when they have something to say. Build a reputation for being accessible. This means never hiding behind closed doors.
- Don't assume that parents understand your words. Someone with lots of time on their hands recently discovered that dictionaries give an average of 28 definitions per word. It's no wonder that different words have different meanings for different people.
- Stay in the here and now. When you are interacting with parents (or anyone else) stay focused in the present moment. Don't let your mind wander. It will show.
- Keep probing until you understand parents' real agenda. What they say isn't always what they are really talking about.
- Your parent public is splintered into many factions lined up on all sides of every school issue. To communicate effectively with all parents, remain neutral. Don't get aligned with any one group—particularly radical groups. For maximum credibility, strive to be comfortable with all groups, but don't get too "cozy" with any of them.
- If school leaders are always coming to parents asking for something (e.g., more money, time, involvement), they eventually get turned off. It helps if you occasionally offer something parents want or need. Some school leaders have gotten a lot of mileage out of issuing a series of Tip Sheets with valuable information parents can use immediately (see Boxes 3.8 and 3.9).

Box 3.8 Parent Tip Sheet

How to Talk to Kids About Sex

- Begin slowly and simply. Often a few sentences are enough for little children. Don't give a full-blown sex education class in response to an innocent question.
- When asked about sex, give answers that suit the child's age.
- Not every question merits a biology lesson.
- Small children don't need too much information or content that is too visual.

If a Young Child "Catches" Parents Having Sex

- Don't overreact.
- Ask what the child saw.
- Explain that grown-ups have special private time together.
- Set boundaries: Next time, knock.
- Make a time for talking to older children about sex.
- Talk about changes (puberty) and new feelings.
- Talk about family values (i.e., respect, honesty, caring).
- Be prepared to answer questions about your own sex life. Don't lie.
- Teach your children to respect other people's space and that "no" means "no."
- Discuss commitment and making good choices.

- Close every parent meeting by restating, outlining, and reviewing (summarizing) the issues discussed.
- To gain parent support, appeal to pride, tradition, and precedent.
- If you are not getting through to parents, ask these questions:
  1. Is my request reasonable and understandable?
  2. Am I using the right words?
  3. What am I leaving out?
  4. Can I give them more choices?
  5. Is there a different/better way to say it?

Box 3.9   Parent Tip Sheet

How to Talk to Kids About Swearing (Profanity)
- Talk to children about the downsides of swearing.
    1. Swearing damages your image and reputation.
    2. Swearing offends many people.
    3. Swearing causes people to lose respect for you.
    4. Swearing indicates you are out of control.
    5. Swearing labels you.
    6. Swearing says you have a limited vocabulary.
    7. Swearing ignores the sensitivity of other people.
    8. Swearing is immature.
    9. Swearing can be hurtful to others.
    10. Swearing doesn't communicate clearly.
    11. Swearing doesn't do any good.
    12. Swearing isn't necessary.
- Point out that "everybody does it" is an excuse, not a justification for swearing.
- Urge your children to learn better ways to handle situations ("cope, not cuss"). Cool people don't need to swear.

Your school is only as good as the parental support it receives. That support is dependent on your ability to inform, instruct, inspire, placate, excite, and rally your parent public.

You have to get your messages across to parents in order to succeed. That's your job as a school leader. If you're good at it, get better. If you don't like it, get over it. If you're not good at it, get to work on it. Let this book help you. Your life doesn't depend on it, but your school does.

4

How to Say the Right Thing to Peers and Colleagues

We're in the same business. We often work in the same building. We may see each other daily. We even share a common jargon. You would think it would be easy for all educators to communicate freely back and forth. Sadly, it doesn't always work that way.

When administrators and teachers communicate, differing agendas, turf battles, suspicion, jealousy, rivalry, false pride, and paranoia sometimes enter in. Even when communicating on the same level, messages don't always get through, because we tend to say what we think the other party wants to hear or what makes us look good. If you think it doesn't happen in your building, look again.

It gets worse. Educators don't talk to each other nearly enough about important topics and issues in the first place. Can you believe it? Professionals, who make their living talking, don't talk to each other enough.

Teachers are pretty much insulated and isolated in their separate classrooms. Principals operate in their solitary role at the building level. And superintendents sit lonely at the top. Where's the dynamic dialogue that characterizes healthy organizations?

When professional educators do talk to each other, much of their communication is merely routine exchanges of information, superficial small talk, gossip, whining, or making excuses. Educators aren't worse about this than other groups. It just matters more because kids are involved.

Too often in schools, what begs to be said and needs to be heard goes unsaid, unheard, and unattended. It doesn't have to be that way. What's needed is more straight talk without fear of reprisal or embarrassment and more meaningful dialogue about kids, teaching, learning, and schools.

Unfortunately, in real life,

- When administrators talk to teachers, they often hold back because they don't want to hurt anyone's feelings, or for fear of backlash from other teachers or union officials.
- When administrators talk to other administrators, they sometimes feel protective of their school or their own image and are reluctant to disclose self-doubts, past mistakes, or serious existing problems.
- When teachers talk to administrators, they naturally hesitate to say anything that would indicate they are less than a master teacher or point out problems or failings that might threaten or upset the administrator.
- When teachers talk to teachers, it's understandable that they may not always want to embarrass themselves by revealing their worst problems or fears to their peers.

It should come as no surprise, then, that many school leaders at all levels even have difficulty asking each other for help, giving advice, criticizing peers or colleagues, complaining about the system's bureaucracy, or giving and receiving compliments.

Most teachers are good at talking to kids. Most principals are good at talking to parent groups. Most superintendents are good at talking to the school board. And most school boards are good at talking to voters and taxpayers.

What would help most, however, is for all of them to learn to talk to each other *openly, honestly, truthfully, thoughtfully,* and *seriously* about matters that matter most. If and when this happens, there's nothing to stop student achievement and the school's ratings from going off the charts. That's what makes this chapter worth reading.

Within the organization, educators usually don't mean to mislead, misinform, misconstrue, or miscommunicate. But it happens too often by default because of ignorance, laziness, bad habits, bad judgment, lack of courage, or because everyone else is doing it. We can do better. Much better.

Meaningful internal dialogue is a prerequisite to any organization's success. It is the first step to collaboration, cooperation, and teamwork. These are also the earmarks of every good school. Who wants anything less?

Straight talk between peers and colleagues should start at the point of first contact—the interviewing and hiring process.

SUCCESSFUL JOB INTERVIEWS: HOW TO ASK THE RIGHT QUESTIONS AND GIVE THE RIGHT ANSWERS

Interviews are the way schools hire people. Business and industry often rely more on psychological profiles, personality exams, and simulation exercises. But the old-fashioned interview is still the selection tool of choice for most schools, even though some are beginning to augment them with classroom photo albums, videotapes, auditions, and teacher licensing tests.

Of course, counting heavily on interviews isn't all bad, because no amount of psychometric data can completely substitute for an eyeball-to-eyeball encounter. Without interviews, there would be no gut reactions or intuitive impressions. And some hall-of-famers would be lost.

The problem with school interviews is that they gauge the candidate's ability to relate to adults, when the successful applicant is really going to be hired to relate to kids. Since these interviews change lives, shape the school now and in the future, and impact students for years to come, it is important to get them right.

Obviously, there are plenty of reasons to say the right thing in interviews. Ask the wrong questions and you may be stuck hiring the wrong person. Give the wrong answers and you may not get a job. That's incentive.

Interviewers need to know the right things to ask, and interviewees need to know how to give on-target responses. Fortunately, there is plenty of advice for those on both sides of the interview table.

It starts with setting the right tone for the interview by being completely honest about the job, its duties, and your expectations. For best results, veteran human resource specialists also recommend that job interviews be structured so that all candidates have an opportunity to respond to identical questions. Hit-and-miss interviews miss more often than they hit.

In order to draw out candidates, skilled interviewers shun yes-or-no questions and instead use a variety of formats including open-ended, reflective, introspective, and situational questions. All inquiries should be job related. Candidates should also be given problems to solve as well as questions to answer.

Some of the best questions deal with values, permit the candidates to showcase their skills, and/or require them to call on examples from real-life experiences (see Box 4.1). To get the full value from the interview, it pays to allow time to probe and ask follow-up questions where appropriate.

Box 4.1   Power Interview Questions

1. Why do you want this job?
2. Describe your leadership (teaching, management) style.
3. What turns you on? Bores you? Makes you mad?
4. What excites you about your daily work?
5. If you weren't an educator, what would you do? Why?
6. What would be your ideal job? Why?
7. What are you best at?
8. What's the hardest thing you've ever had to do?
9. What would your friends tell us about you? What would your enemies tell us?
10. How do kids learn?
11. How should test results be used?
12. What would a visitor see following you around for a day?
13. What do you want as your epitaph?
14. Whom do you admire? Why?
15. How do you keep from getting burned out?
16. What do you expect from a boss (leader)?
17. How do you handle angry parents? Examples?
18. How do you deal with setbacks? Examples?
19. What else should we ask you?
20. Why should we hire you over other candidates?

In the interest of risk management (avoiding costly mistakes and staying out of court), it's also prudent to routinely include certain mandatory interview questions:

- Have you even been convicted of a felony?
- Have you ever been disciplined by a professional organization?
- Are you under court order to pay child support?

Likewise, there are some taboo topics that experienced interviewers scrupulously avoid:

- Citizenship
- National origin

- Pregnancy
- Disabilities
- Economic status
- Home ownership
- Military service
- Number of children
- Public assistance
- Race
- Religion
- Arrest record
- Mental problems

Once the right questions are asked, the real work begins—listening for the right answers and the feelings behind the words. The best advice is to listen carefully for genuine enthusiasm and signs of a built-in affection for kids. These are the essentials. Almost everything else can be learned once the candidate is hired.

Of course, saying the right thing in an interview situation is relatively easy for the interviewer, who has plenty of time to prepare carefully crafted questions. Interviewees, on the other hand, have to be ready for anything. But this doesn't mean that they can't prepare in advance. The following advice can help anyone to say and do the right thing when being interviewed for a teaching or administrative position:

- Do your homework. Learn all you can about the organization and the specific job opening. If possible, have a platform of short- and long-term goals you will pursue if hired.
- Prepare—a lot. Anticipate questions. Rehearse answers. Even polished politicians, including presidents of the United States, rehearse before press conferences.
- Don't bad-mouth or complain about previous bosses or jobs. If the interviewers wanted to hire a whiner, they'd be interviewing two-year-olds.

- Let your passion show. Get excited. Be upbeat, enthusiastic, and willing to learn. That's the kind of employee most schools want to hire.
- Strive to be natural . . . genuine . . . sincere. Good interviewers can spot a phony in the first two minutes—even over the telephone. Be yourself. If they don't want your type, the job wouldn't be a good fit anyway.
- Give specific answers, using real-life examples when possible.
- Take time to think before responding. Ask for clarification if necessary. Never try to guess what the interviewer wants to hear.
- Find ways to highlight your strengths and greatest successes. Tie your experiences to the requirements of the new job.
- Be self-confident, but not arrogant. Don't act like you know it all. You don't. And the interviewer knows it.
- Don't try to be funny, flippant, or cute. It usually comes across as conceited or shallow.
- If asked about something you don't have experience with, counter with your ability to be a "quick study."
- Don't make stuff up. Save your fantasies for your private life. If you don't know an answer, say so.
- Always have a set of questions of your own to ask about the job. (But save queries about salary, benefits, and perks until later.) It's another way to demonstrate your interest in the job.
- Put on your best clothes, your best manners, and your best English for the occasion. Every job interview is a big deal.
- Answer questions with your body, as well as with your words. Make eye contact. Smile. Lean toward the interviewers. Match your gestures to your words. Think of yourself as a total package, not just a talking head.
- Always end with a "thank you" to all who participated in the interview. A follow-up thank-you note adds an extra touch of class as well.

First impressions last. What you say and how you say it in an interview can come back to haunt you and color future communications for a long time to come. That's why interviews should never just happen. They should be carefully choreographed, orchestrated, and prepared for.

The pointers above can help you structure the exchange. Use them to find the right words, ask the right things, or give the right responses the next time (and every time) you are in a job interview situation.

How to Ask for and Offer Help to Peers and Colleagues

People hate to have to ask for help. Educators may be worse than most. People in the education profession see their role as having answers and helping others to become independent and self-sufficient. They are afraid it looks bad if school leaders have to ask for help themselves. What a bunch of hogwash!

Pride is good. False pride is baloney. Everybody needs help sometimes. It's not a cause for shame or embarrassment. It's part of the human condition.

Admitting you need help takes courage. Asking for it is a sign of strength, not weakness. The surprising truth is that people respect people more when they can face reality and seek the help they need.

Helping each other is an expression of humanity. It separates us from most other animals. Asking for help is a form of flattery and friendship. (Most of us don't ask enemies or people we don't like for help.) Being able to give help makes the giver feel good. It also makes it easier to ask for help in return.

As it turns out, asking for help is a win-win situation. So, the next time you need help from a peer or colleague, just ask for it. You'll be glad you did. So will the person you asked.

Once you've overcome self-doubt and false pride, saying the right thing in asking for help is easy. Here's all there is to it:

- Don't hint or drop clues. Spit it out. Simply say, "I need your help to _____" or "Can you help me _____?"
- Be clear. Be specific. Say what you need, why you need it, and when you need it.
- After full discussion and question answering, close the deal. Is it yes or no? You need to know. What's really embarrassing is having to come back and ask a second time.
- Make the helper feel good. That's the fun of it. Show your appreciation. Make it clear how much they helped.
- Don't feel defeated if the other party can't or won't help. There may be a good reason. But nothing's changed. You still need help. Keep asking.

There. That wasn't so bad after all, was it?

The funny thing about helping each other is that most of us feel about as hesitant and awkward in offering help as in asking for it. Again, this is particularly true of educators, who often are afraid they will insult the other party, intrude on another's privacy, or hurt someone's feelings by offering help. This is living proof that even school people can do dumb things. Just how thoughtful, respectful, and helpful can it be to deny offering help to a peer or colleague who really needs it?

If you know or suspect that another school leader needs help, offer it. It's no big deal. At the least, it's a professional courtesy. At best, it's called friendship.

The following do's and don'ts can make offering help a little easier.

Do's
- Offer to do something specific—preferably something only you can do.
- If you can't help, think of someone who can.
- Enjoy the opportunity. Helping others is supposed to feel good.

Don'ts

- Don't just offer vague or generic help. Never just say, "If I can do anything, let me know." Of course you can do something. Just offer outright to do it (calling people, etc.).
- Don't be smug or patronizing in offering your assistance.
- Don't act like a martyr.
- Don't brag about your good deeds.
- Don't keep score.

As school leaders, if we don't help each other, who will? All of us need some kind of help sooner or later. The good news is that it is always available in abundant supply. Getting whatever help you need is as easy (or hard) as asking for it. Just do it.

Reaching out for help and helping others in return is part of doing business as a school leader. That's why they call it a profession.

HOW TO GIVE ADVICE

Don't feel too bad if the temptation to give advice is irresistible; the ability to ignore it is universal.

—Anonymous

We all know fellow administrators and teachers who could use some good advice. We're often reluctant to give it, however, because advice seems to be a commodity that most often goes unused and unappreciated.

Most educators are pretty good at knowing what advice others should follow, but not very good at recognizing the advice they need themselves. Giving advice is a form of helping others, but it works only if it's done right.

The best advice about giving advice is to resist the temptation to rush in and fix things for others—unless and until you are asked. Know when to offer your advice and when to stop. Never push advice off on a reluctant receiver. Give it only when it is requested. Even then, tread carefully.

Not everyone who asks for advice really wants it. Some just want to hear themselves talk. Others only want to hear the advice they already have decided upon. They want validation, not another view.

Before offering any advice, spend a lot of time listening in order to fully understand the choices and issues involved and to ensure that the other party really wants an outside opinion. Listening is the best way to demonstrate your concern and support anyway. When it comes to offering advice, the old adage still rings true—"They won't care what you know, until they know you care."

Even when you are sure that the other party needs and wants your advice, there's a right and a wrong way to give it. The wrong way is to be dogmatic and arrogant about it. The goal should be to help the other person, not to make the person feel inferior or inadequate.

The best way to give advice to peers or colleagues is to let them discover it for themselves. Here's how to do it:

- Ask questions. Raise possibilities. Clarify choices. Don't prescribe.
- Restate the problem as a question and keep reframing the question until the other party identifies his or her own answers.
- Keep reflecting the feelings the other party is expressing. Let the person hear what he or she is really saying.
- Try to point out parallel situations and precedents of what has worked in similar situations in the past.
- Discuss reasons for considering alternative courses of action and the pros and cons associated with each.
- Rather than saying, "You should," say things like, Have you thought about _____? What if _____? Another way would be to _____.

- Make it clear that you will be supportive no matter what choice is made.

To further ensure that advice is actually taken, and taken in the spirit in which it is given, communication specialists suggest that you keep the following six pointers in mind:

1. Never hint at or give advice you don't believe in.

2. If you don't have a clue, don't try to give advice.

3. Limit advice to the areas or subjects asked about.

4. Don't insist or pressure the person to follow your advice. If you do, you'll get the blame if it doesn't pan out. Don't let the other party off the hook that easily. It's still the other person's decision to make.

5. Always include some caveat or disclaimer such as, "My opinion is no better than anyone else's."

6. Don't be hurt if the other person doesn't follow your advice.

Wisdom and experience shouldn't be hoarded. Sharing them is what school leaders do best. Never hesitate to give advice when it is sincerely requested or to take good advice honestly given. It's called teaching and learning.

THE LANGUAGE OF COACHING AND MENTORING

For many school leaders, a powerful source of advice, help, and direction is a mentor or personal coach. The best mentors and coaches help just by knowing the right thing to say at just the right time to make a difference. They put straight talk to work for themselves and others. The tools of mentoring and coaching are simply open-ended questions and a vocabulary of encouragement (see Box 4.2). These are tools you should know about.

Box 4.2   The Language of Mentoring and Coaching

Agenda	Future	Quest
Assumptions	Goals	Reality
Authentic	Growth	Reinvent
Awareness	Habits	Resiliency
Balance	Issues	Satisfaction
Beliefs	Journey	Selfish
Catalyst	Joy	Skills
Change	Knowledge	Spiritual
Choice	Long-term	Strategies
Decisions	Meaningful	Strengths
Desires	Measurable	Talents
Dreams	Needs	Targets
Ethics	Options	Timing
Examine	Overcome	Trade-offs
Expectations	Passion	Understanding
Experiment	Peace of mind	Untraditional
Feelings	Performance	Values
Focus	Plans	Vision
Fulfillment	Priorities	Wake up

All school leaders need at least one good mentor or coach sometime in their career. You probably have had or will have one sooner or later. If you stick around long enough in the profession, you will also probably become a mentor yourself for some other neophyte or wannabe administrator or teacher. You may not even know it at the time.

Mentors are wise and trusted models, teachers, and counselors. Often, they are among the "elders of the tribe." They show protégés the ropes, provide reality checks, facilitate important linkages, connections, and contacts, issue warnings, and steer their wards clear of common career pitfalls.

Mentors don't preach. They teach. They use their experience to make the most of the "teachable moments" that inevitably arise during the daily routine on the job. A good mentor is also a protégé's most enthusiastic cheerleader.

Good mentors don't always have to come from within the profession. You can learn a lot from leaders in other fields as well. Cherish good mentors wherever you find them. Just be sure you do find them.

By contrast, coaches don't judge or give advice. They use guiding and revealing questions to help others examine their careers and lives and to define new life goals (see Box 4.3). Personal coaches ask a lot of leading questions and a few loaded ones until the other person discovers his or her own answer.

Box 4.3   Questions Used by Personal Coaches (Samples)

What would happen if_____?
What do you mean by_____?
Why not_____?
What do you want most?
How do you know that's true?
What's next?
Here's a challenge: _____
What's most important?
What's wrong with this picture?
What would you like to do now?
What do you want to happen?
What do you need right now?
What is your dream?

Personal coaches are usually independent contractors who work with a client for a period of months or years. Their use by executives and leaders in all fields, including education, has grown enormously in recent years. The role of an effective coach is to

- Provide emotional support.
- Remind clients of existing goals. Assist in defining new ones. And help keep the big picture in mind.
- Help clarify what's needed, what's most important, and what's preferred.

- Serve as a sounding board to help clients make wiser decisions and better choices.
- Allow clients to pinpoint what they want most out of life and plan how to get it.
- Limit the client's focus and attention to a few key issues.
- Draw out answers that reveal hidden meanings, agendas, and priorities.
- Motivate and challenge.
- Add power and energy to the direction the client is headed.
- Cause clients to look ahead and define expectations that can become self-fulfilling prophecies.

This is a lot to accomplish with a few choice questions and words of encouragement. But it happens every day. What works for mentors—and coaches—can work for you as well.

You don't have to look too closely to see that the characteristics and techniques of a good mentor or coach are the same as those of any effective school leader. Even if you are not a mentor or coach yourself, once you have mastered the language of mentoring and coaching, you will have gone a long way toward learning how to say the right thing to peers and colleagues in all situations.

If you need more help with this, just get a good mentor or coach of your own.

HOW TO ARGUE AND WIN

All people argue. It's part of daily living and working with others. But school people don't like to argue. They don't like conflict or unpleasantness. They don't like to offend people. They just want things to go along smoothly. So do ostriches.

It's too bad, because there are lots of issues in education and in every school that should be argued about and thrashed out. Unfortunately, many things in our profession that should be said go unsaid, because too many educators have an aversion to honest argument.

The truth is that arguing is a natural human act. Arguments don't have to be nasty, bitter affairs. They can be heated, but civil, exchanges of differing views for the purpose of persuasion. There are bad arguments badly argued. But there are also good arguments that air issues, clarify choices, stimulate thinking, and lead to action. To stifle such arguments is to deny the kind of healthy dialogue that energizes an organization.

No matter how passive or peace-loving you may be, there are times when you have to argue whether you want to or not. That's why it's to your advantage, as a school leader, to learn when to argue, how to argue, and how to win.

Never be afraid to get into an honest difference of opinion or argument with peers or colleagues (or with students, parents, or others). The trick is to learn to argue without malice and without angering or hurting anyone's feelings. The best argument is a "respectful confrontation," not a dogfight.

Sometimes, school leaders shy away from an argument because they're afraid they might lose. They believe that good guys can't win arguments. They're wrong. Anyone can learn to argue and win virtually every time without bullying or becoming mean-spirited.

It starts by giving yourself permission to win. Many people lose arguments simply because they don't let themselves win. If you think you can lose, you are more likely to lose. Assume your case will prevail. Don't just try to win an argument. Make up your mind you are going to win because you are right. Your conviction can become a self-fulfilling prophecy.

Another common fallacy is that arguments are won by superior oratory. The truth is that most arguments are not won by big words, slick phrases, silver-tongued rhetoric, or melodramatic theatrics. Arguments are won by preparation, passion, and plain talk. Period.

Sticking to the truth helps too. The people who win arguments are the ones who are most believable and credible. These are usually the people whose case is closest to the truth.

If you want to argue better, learn when to take a stand and when to walk away. It doesn't make sense to waste time arguing over trifles or in situations where you can't win. If you are going to argue, do it about something substantive.

The next step is to understand the anatomy of a winning argument. Here are the essential components:

- Define the issue.
- Prepare.
- Tell the truth.
- Admit any weaknesses in your case. (This often steals your opponent's thunder.)
- Make it clear what your case is and what outcome you are after.
- Let your passion show. Feelings make a difference. ("No winning argument was ever delivered by the dead or by those imitating the dead." —Gerry Spence).

To flesh out these components, recognized authorities on argumentation offer the following tips that can work for anyone:

- Try to make your case first. Take the initiative. The first statements control the course of the discourse. Counterarguments seldom win.
- Proclaim the truth as you know it. There is no effective rebuttal against it.
- Be honest about your feelings. It will strengthen your believability and credibility. Show emotion. Your bearing, demeanor, and presence are as important as your words. Maybe more.
- In order to sway an audience or convince an opponent, appeal to pity, authority, and/or historical precedent. Whatever works.
- Remain civil and respectful. ("Respect is reciprocal." —Gerry Spence)
- Avoid profanity, sarcasm, ridicule, insults, or cheap shots. And go light on humor. They can cut both ways.

- Use statistics and real information to back up your argument. But avoid overkill. Listeners' eyes glaze over quickly when confronted with too much data.
- Use colorful, descriptive language. Try to create mental images.
- Radiate confidence.
- If the argument is going against your side,
  1. Shift the argument to change the focus.
  2. Slow things down. Resist a rush to judgment.
  3. Seek compromise. Search for common ground.
  4. Get emotional when trying to clinch your argument.

No one can put exact words in your mouth or script an argument for you. But applying these lessons can make it easier for you to find your own words and say the right thing in any argument.

The next time you're in an argument—and I hope you will be in some, because the profession needs them—take these pointers to heart. You will find that good guys can argue and win. There's no argument about it.

THE PROPER ART OF BITCHING: HOW TO COMPLAIN ABOUT THE SYSTEM AND THE PEOPLE IN IT

School personnel complain a lot about the system and the people in it. The trouble is, they complain to their spouse or their carpool or in the lounge. Surprise. Nothing gets better.

Professionals, including school leaders, should point out problems, pinpoint mistakes, and identify what's wrong. That's the way organizations improve.

It doesn't happen enough in schools, however, because too many educators don't want to rock the boat or make anyone mad or get into trouble. They are frequently hesitant to draw attention to themselves by complaining. Timidity is the greatest single obstacle to school improvement. Unfortunately, students sometimes suffer because of the silence.

Without internal critics, organizations get soft and complacent and lose their edge. It can happen in any school. It probably is happening in yours.

It's OK to speak up and complain about what's not working. It's what responsible people do. You should too. And you can once you understand the difference between the right and wrong way to "bitch" about the system.

Of course, the wrong way is to go on a tirade personally attacking whomever you don't like. The wrong way is to criticize people behind their backs. The wrong way is not to take responsibility for anonymous criticism. The only thing worse than silence is anonymity.

The right way to criticize the system—the "proper art of bitching"—isn't as difficult as you might think. Just follow twelve simple, risk-free rules. Don't improvise. Stick to the steps. Here they are:

1. Get all the facts. Get hard evidence. Involve others if appropriate.

2. Follow established channels. If there is a grievance procedure, use it. Be prepared to go to the top. But be sure you're complaining to the right parties. It may not always be the ones listed on the organizational chart. If you're not sure, ask the front office secretaries. They know everything.

3. Be specific. Generalized complaints aren't very useful. Pinpoint precise problems or practices that can be corrected. This is where straight talk comes in.

4. Remain strictly professional. Avoid personal attacks or name-calling. Talk about issues, causes, and consequences, not personalities.

5. Be sure it's a real problem and not just an issue in your mind only.

6. Model civility. Say what needs to be said, but be polite. Don't exaggerate the magnitude of the problem just to make a point. Don't bully. Avoid hysterics.

7. Time your complaint. The time to raise issues is not in the middle of a crisis. Wait until things calm down so people have time to address the problem.

8. Buffer the children. Don't involve kids or let them get caught in the middle of an adult disagreement.

9. Always leave the door open for future talks.

10. Offer to do your part to make things better.

11. Allow time for remedial measures to work. Things didn't get screwed up overnight. They won't get unscrewed immediately, either. But if nothing happens, repeat the process.

12. Don't pout if you don't get your way. Time goes on. There will be other issues. Other triumphs. Other defeats. It's called life.

That's it. The same rules apply whether you're complaining verbally or in writing. Use them to help you find the right words to state your case. Stick with them and you won't get hurt. Better yet, things may actually improve.

Justified criticism isn't negative. It's a form of taking responsibility to help right wrongs and make the organization function better. That's what leadership is all about.

HOW TO CRITICIZE A COLLEAGUE WITHOUT LOSING A FRIEND

If you think it's hard to criticize the "system," it's doubly difficult to criticize a close colleague or friend.

Educators are especially notorious for being reluctant to criticize each other—even when it's constructive criticism. It's even difficult to get them to testify against an incompetent colleague whom everybody knows is doing a lousy job, giving the school a bad name, and hurting kids in the process. There is such a thing as too much loyalty.

No one ever wants to lose a friend, but school leaders, more than most, should know that criticism can be an act of kindness and support when it is done right for the right reasons.

Helping each other to get better and be better is what friends and colleagues are supposed to do. Sometimes, that requires a little "positive confrontation." It's a form of "tough love."

It's always better to confront than to complain behind someone's back or to just let a problem fester while you remain silent about it. Refusing to talk about an issue is not a problem-solving technique.

If you have a beef with a colleague or if the person is doing something seriously wrong that may harm themselves or others, you have an obligation to point it out. Friends don't let friends drink and drive or dig themselves any kind of hole they can't get out of.

The good news is that, in most cases, you can criticize a colleague without losing a friend. Of course, there is always some risk of doing damage to the relationship when you offer criticism, but the stronger the relationship, the smaller the risk.

One essential, preliminary step is to weigh whether a confrontation is worth the small risk and/or if you are the right person to do the confronting. It always pays to consider all possible consequences.

If it is only an isolated issue that bothers you more than anyone else, you may want to bite your tongue and practice tolerance a while longer. But if it is something important that is going to continue and probably get worse, as a school leader, colleague, and friend it's your job to face the situation.

But how? What do you say to a close colleague? How do you say it? Unfortunately, no canned speech will say for you what only you can say for yourself. However, the guidelines below can point you in the right direction, set you up for success, and help you say the right thing whenever you have to criticize or confront a colleague:

- Rehearse. Practice in advance. Visualize how the confrontation may play out. Be prepared for varying reactions.
- Choose the right time and place. A private setting is usually best.
- Begin by acknowledging and affirming the friendship. Say something like, "I wouldn't say this if I didn't think so much of you" or "Since we're such close friends, I feel an obligation to tell you _____."
- Don't launch into a verbal attack. Separate criticism from viciousness or vindictiveness. Avoid shouting, no matter how angry you are.
- Don't be moralistic or judgmental. You're supposed to be helping, not playing judge and jury.
- Pinpoint specific behavior(s). Cite specific examples and incidents.
- Try to use positive word choices. Don't pick the harshest descriptors you can think of. Be truthful, but be respectful. Use plain words—not hurtful ones.
- Make it clear that you value the person and the relationship. It's the behavior that is the problem.
- Talk about feelings. Your feelings. Your colleague's feelings. Others' feelings. Often, people don't realize how their behavior makes others feel.
- Use a firm, nonthreatening voice.
- Think about your body language. Straight-on eye contact is best when delivering constructive criticism.
- Listen carefully to what the person has to say. You may learn something that will change your mind or modify your criticism.
- Work with your colleague to search for solutions, alternatives, or compromises.
- Pledge your support to help change things and follow through on your promise.

Criticizing a colleague is never easy. But sometimes it is necessary. However, it doesn't have to cost you a friendship if you follow the steps above. On the few occasions when a relationship doesn't survive a little well-intentioned criticism, it probably wasn't a viable friendship anyway.

As a school leader, if you are honest, you will praise colleagues when appropriate. If you are honest, you will also criticize colleagues when appropriate. If you are not honest, you shouldn't be a school leader to start with.

What to Say and Not Say When Giving References and Recommendations

It has always been a tough task to write references and recommendations for colleagues and employees. There are several inherent problems and conflicts of interest that make it difficult.

If you are writing recommendations for good employees, you naturally want to keep them, but you also want to be supportive of their chances for advancement. If the employees are marginal, you might like to get rid of them, but you don't want to dump them on another unsuspecting employer. Oy vey! What do you say?

Every school leader has wrestled with these issues and the questions of what to say, how much to say, how to say it, and what not to say in employee recommendations. At best, reference writing has been a challenge.

Well, it just got a lot more challenging. With the advent of today's court-conscious society where lawsuits are as prevalent as the common cold, educators, at all levels, have become increasingly paranoid about sharing anything in writing about anyone else. You can't actually blame them.

Many reference-writers are now hesitant to say too many good things for fear of backlash if the person doesn't pan out in the new job. Likewise, they are equally afraid to say too much that is negative, because the candidate may file a nuisance lawsuit if the job goes to someone else. The result is an epidemic of wishy-washy, noncommittal references that don't say much to help either employees or employers. So much for straight talk.

Many school personnel are so leery of getting into trouble that they have adopted a "name, rank, and serial number mentality." When asked for a recommendation, they divulge only the employee's dates of employment, work assignment, and stated reason for leaving. Of course, this is accurate and truthful information, but it is not very useful to prospective employers.

Fortunately, there are some practical guidelines that make it possible to write honest, helpful recommendations and stay out of court. The do's and don'ts below show how to sort out what to include and not include when making recommendations for colleagues today:

Do's

- Stick to facts. Include only information that is observable, documented, or a matter of public record.
- Be descriptive. Use actual examples.
- Choose words carefully. Avoid superlatives.
- Limit statements of opinion, particularly if they are negative. If you do express opinions, clearly label them.
- If you want to promote the employee, cite any awards or honors received, win-loss records, or any other documented achievements.
- Be eloquent (loud and clear in what you don't say).
- Consult with legal counsel if you have questions.

Don'ts

- Include anything that you can't document or prove.
- Make reference to any rumors, allegations, or gossip about the employee.
- Divulge anything that can't be legally asked about in a job interview.
- Put anything in writing that you wouldn't say to the person's face.

- Go into an employee's personal problems or medical history. Likewise, don't share confidential reviews or letters of reprimand.
- Be intentionally vague. Statements such as "I cannot recommend this employee too highly" lend themselves to varied interpretation.
- Lie. If the employee is a jerk, don't pass him or her off as a superstar.

For further help on what to say and how to say it when recommending colleagues, see the sample letters (one for a good employee in Box 4.4 and one for a marginal employee in Box 4.5).

Box 4.4   Sample Letter of Recommendation for a Good Employee

---

Dear_____:

In response to your request, I am happy to write a letter of recommendation on behalf of Ms. X.

Ms. X has taught advanced placement history courses in our high school for the past five years. During that time, she also served as Student Council adviser and coached the Varsity debate team. Last year Ms. X was selected by the local Chamber of Commerce as Outstanding Teacher of the Year.

Ms. X has been very popular with students and parents as evidenced by over 100 unsolicited letters of commendation received by our office in the last year alone. Over that same period, we have received no complaints about her work.

Naturally, I would hate to lose Ms. X, but I am confident that she would be a welcome addition to any staff. Without reservation, I can recommend her for any position for which she is licensed.

Sincerely,

_____

Box 4.5   Sample Letter of Recommendation
for a Marginal Employee

Dear_____:

This letter is in response to your request for a recommendation for Ms. Y.

Ms. Y was employed by our district as a Middle School English teacher from 2006 to 2008. She is also licensed to teach social studies. As stated in her letter of resignation, she left our employment for "personal reasons."

During her period of employment, Ms. Y's attendance record was satisfactory.

I wish Ms. Y well in her future plans.

Sincerely,

_____

In today's litigious culture, school leaders can't always say everything they might want to say when writing recommendations for colleagues. But, as illustrated in the sample letters, they can still say enough right things to get their message and meaning across to prospective employers.

It behooves school officials to take writing recommendations seriously. A single letter of reference may change a life or influence a school's future for years to come. Write them carefully. Then, just hope that some other school leader will be equally conscientious when writing a letter of recommendation for you if you ever need one.

What to Say and How to Say It in Performance Reviews

Writing recommendations is hard. Writing performance reviews is even harder. It's harder because everyone gets one, so feelings and morale are affected. Jobs and careers hang in the balance. Promotions are based on them. So are terminations. Performance reviews have to be done right.

On the surface, performance reviews appear somewhat cut-and-dried. Many use a checklist. That's the easy part. It's the written stuff that accompanies the checklists that gets tricky.

There's nothing complicated about the format of a typical job evaluation. A good performance review merely examines the past, defines the present, and charts the future. Most consist of only three basic components:

1. Strengths—what the evaluatee is doing right

2. Areas for improvement—what the evaluatee needs to do better

3. Action plans—suggestions for improvement. (Often these are nonnegotiable expectations tied to a specific timeline.)

The problem is that filling in the blanks is a lot more difficult than it looks. There are lots of things to think about in developing a fair, accurate, and meaningful performance review.

Fortunately, you don't have to think of them all by yourself. They are all laid out in the list of commonsense rules below. Follow them faithfully and you'll end up saying the right things in the right way every time—or close enough to get the job done.

Rules for Performance Reviews

1. Base evaluations on multiple, firsthand observations. Be sure you know what you are looking for in advance.

2. Don't put anything in writing you wouldn't say face-to-face.

3. Be honest and direct. Don't skirt tough issues. Say what has to be said and say it plainly.

4. Describe what you've seen. Give evidence and examples. Cite specific, observable behaviors. Remember that you are assessing performance, not personality.

5. Evaluate the right things. Don't focus unduly on extremes. Avoid being swayed by peaks and valleys of performance. Concentrate on the employee's average performance over time. Careers aren't made out of isolated, singular events. They are built systematically by taking care of business every day.

6. Define terms if necessary. Be sure the evaluatee thoroughly understands everything said in the evaluation.

7. Where appropriate, compare the employee's productivity with others. A performance review is like a report card for adults.

8. Start out being general and become more specific as you go on.

9. Be complete. Include the good, the bad, and the ugly—especially the good. We all need a little authentic praise from superiors.

10. Identify both skills needing improvement and new skills to be learned.

11. Don't just look backward. Ask, "What have you done for me lately?" Look ahead. Set goals.

12. Clearly identify and label all statements of opinion.

13. Choose words carefully (see Box 4.6). As always, the overriding goal is clarity.

14. Strike a balance. Don't skimp on relevant facts, but don't include too much information either. A performance review is supposed to be a working, workable document, not a New York City phone book.

15. Never write a job evaluation when you're angry or use it as a threat or a punishment.

16. Don't include rumors, accusations, or allegations.

17. Refrain from moralizing or sermonizing.

18. Beware of the halo effect. Don't let unusually good or bad behavior in one area color your perception of overall performance.

19. Include all areas of deficiency. Cite any policy violations.

20. Look at trends. Are things getting better? Worse?

21. Include standards, deadlines, and benchmarks as appropriate.

22. Vary verbiage so that all job evaluations don't sound canned or look exactly alike. Cookie-cutter appraisals don't work.

23. Spell out what you and others will do to help the employee reach improvement goals.

24. Give the evaluatee adequate time to explain or offer rebuttal.

25. Always end with an action plan. Communicate expectations clearly and concisely. Leave no room for misinterpretation. Match timelines for improvement to the difficulty of the task. Some improvements, such as showing up on time, can be made starting tomorrow morning. Others may take weeks or months.

26. Affirm your belief that the employee can "make it." And pledge your help.

27. Always follow up every performance review with periodic progress checks.

Box 4.6　Power Words for Performance Reviews

Absenteeism	Follow through	Profanity
Accountability	Goal setting	Professional
Achievement	Habits	Punctuality
Adjust	Hygiene	Recognize
Assess	Identify	Record keeping
Attend	Immediate	Reform
Avoid	Implement	Refrain
Awareness	Improvement	Remedial
Become	Initiate	Report
Behavior	Introduce	Require
Carry out	Knowledge	Respect
Communication skills	Leadership	Responsibility
Comply	Learn	Safety
Cooperate	Limit	Satisfy
Courses	Mandate	Self-assessment
Deadline	Measurable	Stop
Demonstrate	Mentor	Support
Desist	Model	Teamwork
Develop	Network	Time use
Display	New	Training
Emphasize	Ordered	Understand
Encourage	Participate	Upgrade
Exhibit	Plan	Value
Familiarize	Prepare	Work ethic
Feedback	Present	
Focus	Probation	

If you are like most school leaders, you prepare lots of performance reviews each year. To expedite the process, it pays to develop a compilation of standard phrases that can be plugged into individual action plans as appropriate.

It's possible to buy such lists, but they never quite sound like what you would really say or how you would actually say it. They always sound manufactured (mass produced), which corrupts the integrity of the evaluation. That's why it's better to develop your own collection, using your own words (see Box 4.7). It's more work, but it's a one-time-only project that you can add to or modify as time goes by.

Box 4.7   Sample Phrases for Performance Reviews

- Must follow daily cleaning schedule as outlined by the director of Maintenance.
- Needs to develop more flexible (varied) lesson plans to accommodate a variety of learning styles.
- Needs to upgrade computer skills in the area of word processing. The district will pay for appropriate training, which must be completed by June 30.

It's not necessary to write every performance review entirely from "scratch." But to be effective, each one should contain some "fresh" writing based on the unique circumstances involved.

Properly done, a performance review capsulizes performance without springing any surprises. This isn't easy. That's why no one enjoys writing them. Nevertheless, they seem to be a necessary nuisance in schools, because everyone needs feedback.

Good employees need affirmation, validation, encouragement, reinforcement, and an occasional nudge. Weak employees need a wake-up call or a kick in the pants periodically. They won't get better all by themselves.

You may not like to do it, but you can learn how to write effective, no-nonsense performance reviews that get the intended messages across to all employees. That's why we have books like this. That's why you are reading this one. It really can help you say the right thing in every job evaluation you write if you let it. Let it.

How to Pay Tribute to a Colleague

It's easy to understand why it's hard to advise, criticize, or evaluate a colleague. But honoring or recognizing a co-worker in public should be a piece of cake. Right? Not necessarily.

Paying tribute to a colleague can be awkward. You don't want to say too much. Of course, you don't want to say too little either. You don't want to sound phony, insincere, too mushy, or over-the-top. You want to say just the right thing. But what is that?

Educators often make expressing tribute more awkward and complicated than it should be. The trick is to simply state why you're there, why the person deserves recognition or congratulations, how you feel about the honoree, and what he or she has done, then stop. That's it.

Here are some other tips that can help you pull it off:

- Be timely. Don't wait too long to recognize accomplishments or the tribute will be anticlimactic.
- Be genuine. If you don't honestly like, honor, or respect the person, let someone else do it.
- Be sure listeners understand why you are honoring the person. Use examples of specific acts and incidents.
- Talk about the honoree as a person—not an icon.
- Let your emotions come through. State how you feel. Tell how happy and thrilled you are to be able to honor the person. Express admiration and pride.
- Use traditional words of respect and tribute (see Box 4.8).
- Try to say something that shows your unique or personal connection to the honoree—something that only you can say.
- Don't eulogize the honoree. The person is being recognized, not buried.
- Don't compare the honoree's accomplishments to someone else's.
- Don't qualify or limit the honoree's achievement. Don't infer that the person's success was due to luck or try to steal some of the credit for yourself.
- Don't act surprised that the honoree was successful.
- Be brief. We're talking paragraphs, not pages.
- Close with best wishes for continued success.

Box 4.8   Words of Tribute

Accolades	Hero	Respected
Accomplishment	Honor	Role model
Achievement	Humility	Sacrifice
Admire	Impressive	Service
Applause	Innovative	Significant
Awesome	Inspiration	Skilled
Beloved	Joy	Special
Caring	Knowledgeable	Success
Celebration	Leader	Super
Commend	Magnificent	Talent
Contribution	Neat	Tribute
Credit	Old-fashioned	Unequaled
Dedicated	One-of-a-kind	Unforgettable
Example	Outstanding	Unique
Excellence	Pillar	Unrivaled
Exceptional	Pleased	Unselfish
Extraordinary	Praise	Unusual
Fantastic	Prize	Valued
Great	Proud	Well-deserved
Hard-working	Record-breaking	Wisdom
Hats off	Remembered	Wonderful

It can be easy to say nice things about a colleague or co-worker if you follow the "3 B's":

- Be yourself
- Be sincere.
- Be succinct.

The more you get out of yourself and into the other person's achievement, the easier it is.

The next time you have to pay tribute to a colleague, don't worry. Just think less abut how you're going to sound and more about why the person deserves recognition, and you'll say the right thing every time.

How to Say the Right Thing
to the Central Office

Any organization is only as strong as its two-way, internal communication. You might prefer not to communicate very much with head office personnel. You may not want to bother your bosses. You may be afraid of being perceived as kissing up to your superiors. You may not want to draw attention to your building's or department's problems. It doesn't matter.

It's still your responsibility to communicate freely and frequently with the central office. More important, it's to your advantage. You can't get noticed if you don't interact with the district office. Likewise, you can't get help, direction, support, or special resources from district office personnel if they never hear from you.

If you are concerned about what to share with the head office, how to share it, or what to keep to yourself, there are a few do's and don'ts that can help clear it up. Let's start with the don'ts.

To avoid communication mix-ups or mishaps with the district office,

- Don't wait for district administrators to initiate all the communications. They want to hear from you too. Even central office personnel can feel isolated, cut off, or left out.
- Don't bother front office personnel with trifles or too much small talk. Even if you wonder what they do all day, they are busy people too.
- Don't tell them all your troubles. Being a school leader means being a problem-solver. That takes more than merely passing problems up the ladder. If you can't handle your share of problems without calling on the district office for help, you're not keeping your part of the bargain.
- Don't exaggerate the magnitude of your issues, problems, mistakes, or successes.
- Don't forward gossip or perpetuate rumors.
- Don't play games by censoring, withholding, or slanting information to suit your purposes.
- Don't attempt to play politics or manipulate people.
- Don't ask for unfair advantage or curry favors.

- Don't gloat over temporary victories. It may be premature, and then you'll look foolish.
- Don't try to show off how hip you are by using the latest buzzwords. You may only embarrass yourself by being caught using yesterday's catchwords.
- Don't try to discredit the successes of other administrators, buildings, or departments.
- Don't take credit that belongs to someone else.
- Don't lie to the central office. It's the kiss of death if and when the truth comes out.

So much for what won't work. Below are proven guidelines and strategies that do work in determining what to share with the district office and how to share it:

- Find out whom you really need to communicate with for different purposes. This means learning both the formal and informal power structure of the superintendent's cabinet. The real movers and shakers aren't always who you think they are. Your communications won't be productive if you are not talking to the right people.
- Find out how district administrators want to receive information. Get to know their individual communication styles so that you can adapt your style to theirs (see Box 4.9).
- Alert district administrators to pending or potential problems. They will appreciate not being blindsided.
- Share good news. Don't just run to the front office when there's trouble. They will get tired of seeing you coming.
- Praise, compliment, and thank district office personnel when appropriate. They don't get many warm fuzzies either.
- Make friends with district office secretaries. They can tip you off about how to get through, how to get the right party's ear, and how to get what you want.

Box 4.9   Preferred Communication Styles

---

1. Visual
   - Prefers written instructions, directions, and explanations.
   - Likes schematics, diagrams, and flowcharts.
   - Responds to specific examples.

2. Auditory
   - Prefers to receive information orally.
   - Likes to listen.
   - Responds to discussions and oral presentations.

3. Kinesthetic (Tactile)
   - Prefers to learn by doing.
   - Likes to "get a handle" on new information.
   - Responds to hands-on experiences.

- Build a relationship of trust over time so that you can be honest when you need to be.
- Change your communication strategy as central office personnel changes. New personalities may require a new approach.
- Be assertive, but not pushy or obnoxious. There are no trophies for timidity.
- Be brave enough to be candid about what's working and what's not. It may not be what district administrators want to hear, but it is what they need to know.
- Consider giving the central office a weekly or monthly update from your building or department.
- If necessary, break bad news gradually, but tell the whole story before someone else does.
- Be mostly positive and upbeat. If you consistently have a chip on your shoulder, the central office may tune you out.
- Be willing to state where you stand and what you stand for.

- Do whatever it takes to get district office personnel into your building so you can have face-to-face communication on your own turf.
- If you're making a hard sell, communicate with district office team members individually, rather than as a group.
- Volunteer to take on extra responsibilities. It gets you noticed and makes it harder for central administrators to avoid listening to what you have to say.
- Be willing to disagree with district personnel without being disagreeable. If you always are a yes-man (or woman), they know you're phony. Besides, if everyone always agrees, some are useless. It could be you.
- Be politically correct in all communications with the central office.
- Remember your etiquette.
- Use self-deprecating humor to defuse tense situations.
- Know when to lie low and not say anything. (When the stuff hits the fan, it is not distributed equally. You want to be out of the way.)

The district office administrators don't need to know everything. There are a few things it's even better that they don't know about. Then, there's everything else. It's your job to broker this information to see that district personnel get what they want and need to know as well as what you want them to know about.

In addition to the considerations above, timing is crucial to effective communication with the main office. The best advice about timing is simply, "If it's good news, get it out quick. If it's bad news, get it out quicker" (—*The District*).

HOW TO SAY THE RIGHT THING TO THE SCHOOL BOARD

It should be no surprise that communicating with the school board (Board of Education) may entail some special considerations. If you are a principal, all of the previous tips apply. If you are a superintendent, however, additional pointers require attention.

Never play favorites in communicating with school board members. Only a naïve or foolhardy superintendent favors some board members with more or different information than is given to all members. As leader of the school, it is imperative that you give all the board all of the information needed to make sound decisions (not just what members want to hear). It also pays to risk being repetitive or redundant to ensure that all members "get it." Likewise, be slavish to the truth. There is never a good enough reason to hoard or withhold information, purposely distort information, or provide false information to individual members or to the board as a whole.

Of course, exactly what you communicate to the board and how you convey it depends, in part, on your vision of the role of the superintendent. If, like me, you believe that part of the job is to educate and even occasionally discipline the board, you will tailor your communications accordingly. However, if you think the job is merely to "serve" the board, your approach will differ.

In any event, it is important to be respectful and professional in all communications with board members. Don't gossip. Respect confidentialities. And never bully or patronize the board. Finally, try to avoid arguing with board members in public and be sure to give the board some credit for all school successes.

In summary, communication is the lifeblood of every school system. Free-flowing information sharing up and down the ladder is crucial to success. That's where you come in. As a school leader, you had better be good at it or find out how to get good at communicating. It's the most important thing you do every day.

In addition to all the other advice in this chapter, there is one more thing you should know about communicating with peers and colleagues at all levels. When in doubt, talk to them as you would want to be talked to. The right thing to say to others is always what you would want to hear yourself in that situation. It's that simple.

It's the Golden Rule in action. It works so well, it's a wonder that everyone doesn't follow it. Yet, in over 2,000 years, we haven't gotten it. Get it now.

It bears repeating. Applying the Golden Rule is the single best way to ensure saying the right thing to colleagues (or anyone else for that matter) in every situation. Most people know this. Effective leaders actually do it.

5

How to Say the Right Thing to the General Public and the Media

Schools exist because the public supports them. If communities don't believe in their schools and support them financially and otherwise, educational excellence is out of the question. Even mediocrity is a long shot.

The problem is that most of the public don't really know what it's like in schools today. Some think they do because they went to school once—probably many years ago. But they actually don't have a clue.

Most adults haven't been inside a school for more than a few hours in years. In many communities, the majority of residents don't even have kids in school. The only thing most community members know about their schools is what they hear from their kids, school spokespersons, and the media.

Since the media focus mostly on the sensational (i.e., gangs, drugs, bomb scares, school shootings, teen sex, low test scores, and sports), this places a heavy burden on school leaders to say the right thing to effectively tell the school's story and to maintain public support. Are you up to it?

You can be if you master a few fundamentals. When communicating with the public or the media about your schools, there are a multitude of ways to do it wrong. (You'll read about most of them in the pages ahead.) But this chapter is designed to help you find the right ways. It starts by realizing that you're never completely "off the record" and that even small talk in social situations can have big consequences.

SMOOTH SCHMOOZING: HOW TO MAKE SMALL TALK

We all gotta talk.
—Larry King

Man is the talking animal. Public figures—including school officials—have to talk more than most. It's their stock in trade.

As a school leader, your job includes participating in countless informal, social, and ceremonial events that require making small talk and conducting ordinary, casual conversations with all facets of the public. Even when principals and superintendents are "off duty," they are perceived as representatives of the school.

Like it or not, how you conduct and present yourself in everyday conversational situations can influence what people think about the schools. Strangely enough, many members of the public listen more closely to what you say "off the cuff" than to any of your formal or official statements. If you come across in conversation as confident and upbeat, that image often carries over to the school in many people's minds. On the other hand, if you appear nervous, confused, tentative, and ill at ease, people walk away with a little less faith in the schools.

It may not be fair, but it's the real world for school administrators in most communities. That makes it important to be conscious of saying the right thing all the time. Effective school leaders have to know how to make small talk, schmooze with all kinds of people, and "work the room" at social affairs.

Of course, not all educators find it easy to talk readily with strangers or are comfortable in all social situations. Some are shy. You may be one of them. (Yes, school personnel are allowed to be shy. Actually, 80% of the population is or has been shy sometime in their lives.)

Don't despair. Shyness isn't a terminal illness. Socializing is an acquired behavior. Anyone can learn to schmooze with the best of them. If you need to and want to, you can get better at approaching groups, starting conversations, and keeping them going in a way that presents you (and the school) in the best possible light.

If you are not a skilled schmoozer, you're not alone. Most people aren't. But they can be. The trick is to have faith in yourself, use listening as a tool to get started, and pay more attention to what others are thinking, feeling, and saying than to what you want to say.

The key to smooth schmoozing is listening. It is the quickest, easiest way to get free information about other people, learn their "hot buttons," and identify possible conversation topics. Listening intently can make you a popular conversationalist without ever opening your mouth.

To make listening work to your advantage, do what the best listeners do: (a) ask open-ended questions; (b) echo or paraphrase the speaker's points; (c) check frequently for understanding; (d) maintain reasonable eye contact (too much eye contact feels like "visual stalking"); (e) watch for nonverbal clues and cues; and (f) concentrate on really hearing and remembering what is said. Once you become a skilled listener, you are well on your way to mastering the art of making small talk.

Schmoozing is a dance. If possible, you want to lead. The first step at any social event is to appear approachable by maintaining an open position. If people don't come to you, go to them. Here's how:

- Select a convenient group.
- Hover and eavesdrop for a few minutes.
- Show interest in what's being said.
- Make eye contact with one or two in the group.
- Wait for an appropriate break in the action and symbolically ask for permission to join the group by saying something like, "May I ask a question?" or "Are you talking about last night's ball game?"

Voila! You're in the stream of conversation.

A variation is to start the dance by approaching a single individual. Be the first to say "Hello." Sociologists tell us that people then have between seven and ten seconds to make a positive first impression.

This allows just about enough time for an effective ritual greeting including a friendly salutation (7–10 words, something simple like, "I'm _____. Is this your first time here?", a firm handshake, a smile, eye contact, and a chance to hear and repeat the person's name.

The next movement in the dance is to keep the conversation going by asking questions about the other person (e.g., "How long have you lived here?" or "How many children do you have?"), revealing more specific information about yourself, and talking about things around you. At this point, it's best to stick to "safe topics" (see Box 5.1).

Box 5.1   Safe Conversation Topics

Traffic

Weather

Arts

Calendar of events

Sports

News

Family

Once a connection has been made, you can pep up the conversation by pursuing some of the other party's interests or sharing more personal experiences, ideas, or opinions. Then, you're on your own. Keep listening for more clues on where to steer the conversation next.

Other suggestions that can boost your schmooze power include these tips:

- Check your attitude at the door. Keep the conversation positive.
- Stand straight. It makes you feel more confident. Posture is an outward measure of power.
- Focus on other people, rather than talking about yourself. "Themselves" is everyone's favorite topic of conversation. It always pays to make others feel important.
- Avoid surefire conversation killers (see Box 5.2).
- Act interested. Be animated. Show enthusiasm.
- Don't drink alcohol to bolster your self-confidence. Charm is not a function of chemicals.
- Politely avert controversial questions or discussions about the schools while in a social setting. Avoid dealing with individual school problems. Take a tip from doctors and lawyers who don't give out free advice over cocktails.

- Keep sending receptive signals (e.g., leaning toward the speaker, looking at whoever is talking, keeping an open stance) throughout the conversation.
- If the momentum begins to lag, you can always fall back on the one guaranteed conversation-saving question, "Why?"

Box 5.2   Conversation Stoppers

Bragging
Put-downs
Inattentive listening
Argumentative statements
Flirting
Gossiping
Rude or crude language
Laughing inappropriately
Gross examples
Interrupting
Bad-mouthing others
Sexist or racist remarks
Sexual innuendos
Profanity
Blatant manipulation

You don't need any more rules than that to find the right words, say the right thing, and handle conversation in any social setting. The only other requirements are to relax, have fun, and go with the flow.

In social dance classes, they always teach that how you end the dance is as important as how you start it. The same applies to schmoozing and making small talk. It's not always easy to end or break away from a conversation without appearing rude, brusque, or disinterested.

That's why some experts offer the following four steps for disengagement from a group or individual:

1. Break physical contact.

2. Turn partially away and begin to pull back while showing you are still listening.

3. State your reason for moving on ("I have to use the bathroom" always works).

4. Leave. Don't wait for permission to go. Don't look back.

Obviously, making small talk at social events, at the market, or on the street corner is not the most important thing you do as a school administrator. But it isn't chopped liver either. It deserves some conscious attention.

Informal conversations allow you to establish rapport with parents and citizens, line up allies, gauge public feelings on issues, identify sore spots in the making, defuse concerns before they become complaints, and make a good impression that can translate into better feelings about the school. All that is worthwhile work.

The point is to realize that small talk is often more than it appears to be. It is important to try to say the right thing even in casual contacts without becoming uptight or paranoid about it.

No small talk is necessarily wasted time and effort. Sometimes, it can even be a tool for changing minds, selling ideas, and molding public opinion.

HOW TO SWAY OPINION AND PERSUADE NONBELIEVERS

All communications have a purpose. Some are intended to inform or instruct. Some are merely for entertainment, and some are expressly designed to sell something, change minds, sway opinion, and convince naysayers. In case you haven't noticed, the latter category makes up much of what you do every day as a school leader.

If you don't think of yourself as a salesperson, you're missing the point of much of your job. Whether it's trying to get kids to avoid dugs, parents to accept a new bus schedule, teachers to adopt a new curriculum, the school board to fund a favorite project, or the entire community to vote for a referendum, it's selling. If the public quits buying what you're selling, you're not leading anymore—you're only making do. It makes you want to become the best salesperson you can be, doesn't it?

To succeed as an educator today you need to know how to say and do the right thing to convince or persuade people to accept your ideas. There are lots of practical and professional ways to do it. You already know many of them. You can learn the rest. Fortunately, they are easy; they don't require any special training, and they usually work.

Much of what it takes to be persuasive is laid out in the section on "How to Argue and Win" in Chapter 4. The following paragraphs will fill in the gaps. The first thing you need to know about persuasion is that it requires

- The right product (idea)
- The right people (target audience)
- The right timing

All good salespeople know that they have to start with a good product. It works the same way in schools. You shouldn't have to go to sales classes to know that if you start with a half-baked idea, an ill-conceived program, or a bond issue whose time has not yet come, you're sunk before you get on board. Don't try to sell a bad idea. It's hard enough to sell a good one.

Once you have the right produce (idea), be sure you're selling it to the right people—the people who can make it happen. Don't waste time persuading sixth graders that you have a great idea if only the school board has the power or authority to approve it.

Even with a good product and the right audience of potential buyers, successful selling requires good timing. If there is no more money in the bank, no amount of salesmanship is going to convince the school board to fund a new project. It's bad timing. One law of persuasion is to be patient when the time isn't right and be persistent when it is.

Once you have the right product, the right people, and the right timing, the process of persuasion usually follows certain sequential steps:

1. Get the target audience to *pay attention* to your message. Get it on their radar screen and hook it to their interests.

2. Get them to *understand* your message. It pays to use examples from your audience's life experiences.

3. Get them to *believe* your message. Use energy, evidence, and enthusiasm. This is the pivotal point in the process.

4. Get them to *retain* your message. This is the time for repetition and reinforcement.

5. Get them to *act* on your message. You will get action only if you directly ask for it.

To negotiate these steps successfully requires a combination of tact and tactics. The most persuasive school leaders you know employ a variety of strategies to "sell" their ideas, shape opinion, and convince nonbelievers, such as

- Have a clear vision of your purpose, your case, your audience, and your method of delivery before you start.
- Be credible. Say what you mean. (Remember straight talk?) Good salespeople sell themselves first and their product second.
- Arouse sympathy where appropriate. Present facts. Show passion.

- Develop a clear and simple message and stick to it. Slogans still work in today's "sound-bite society."
- Appeal to your audience's needs (e.g., fears, emotions, higher calling, sense of justice, etc.).
- Use persuasive power words (see Box 5.3).
- Continuously emphasize the benefits for your audience.
- Use whatever works for your side (e.g., statistics, expert opinion, historical precedent).
- Stick to the truth. It will never get you into trouble.
- Allow feedback. Listen to suggestions and adjust your case as needed. Soliciting input has become a central component of all communications today.
- Act like you know what you are doing and talking about no matter what happens.
- Resist the urge to oversell.

Box 5.3   Persuasive Power Words

Adaptable	Efficient	Productivity
Advantage	Encourage	Proven
Affordable	Evidence	Quickest
Appealing	Exciting	Responsible
Authentic	Expert opinion	Results
Benefit	Extraordinary	Safer
Best	Factual	Selling points
Better	Fastest	Smart
Breakthrough	Feasibility	Solid
Cheaper	Features	Sound
Convenient	Genuine	State-of-the-art
Convincing	Innovative	Successful
Cost-effective	Interesting	Superior
Dependable	Money-saving	Testimonials
Desired	Overwhelming	Unfailing
Detailed	Popular	Unusual
Doable	Powerful	User-friendly
Economical	Practical	Well-thought-out
Effective	Proactive	

The last, best advice on persuasion and opinion molding is to take one more page from the sales manual. The real champions in the world of selling know that

- All salespeople tell.
- Good salespeople explain.
- Great salespeople show how it works.

Think about it. It's a lesson that can help you sway opinion and persuade nonbelievers as a school leader.

No successful salesperson works from a prepared sales pitch. They prefer to use their knowledge of what works to tailor-make their presentation to fit each individual situation. That's how this chapter can help you say the right thing when it comes time to convince the skeptics in your community.

All of the skills and techniques for changing people's minds and turning around opinion presented above can also come in handy when dealing with criticisms and complaints.

HOW TO HANDLE COMPLAINTS FROM THE PUBLIC

Even Jesus got complaints. School leaders should expect nothing less. After all, complaints are a natural by-product of managing a public institution in a democracy. The good news is that complaints are only what you make of them. They can be booby traps, tests, challenges, or opportunities. It is the response to the complaint that determines what it finally becomes.

The ability to say the right thing to defuse complaints spells the difference between alienating a patron and escalating a concern or salvaging an ally by solving a problem. Believe me, salvaging and solving are better. That's why this section is designed to help you make save-the-day responses to everyday complaints from the public.

Every school system has its share of dissatisfied pupils, parents, and patrons who are not shy about voicing their displeasure. Yours is no exception.

Some complaints are legitimate and justified. Some are not. All deserve a personal response. More often than not, this is an administrator's job.

Most people with complaints want to deal with someone in a position of authority, someone who can really do something about the problem. That's why good school leaders have to be good "customer" complaint officers.

Dealing with complaints is never easy or fun, but each one is an opportunity to resolve an issue, right a wrong, convince a skeptic, or save a valuable relationship that is in jeopardy of being severed.

It never pays to downplay, ignore, or deny complaints. How you deal with upset patrons says a lot about how effective you are as a school leader.

The secret to successful complaint resolution is to take every complaint seriously. Even if it is simply a misunderstanding or a mistake by the other party, every complaint demands personal attention. What appears petty to you may seem significant to the offended party. If a complaint is important to even one of your constituents, it's important. Period! Treat it accordingly.

Complaints aren't just nuisances or inconveniences. You don't get complaints because of bad luck. You get them because of bad performance. They can be valuable warning signs.

Most complaints are merely problems put into words. Without them, glitches, weak links, or other difficulties can easily go unnoticed, undetected, and unresolved until serious problems result. More often than not, complaining pupils or patrons are messengers, not troublemakers.

Unfortunately, problems don't solve themselves. Someone has to fix them. It often doesn't happen until there's a complaint. People who complain about your schools may be doing you a favor. Effective school leaders learn from the complaints they receive. Your goal should be to never get the same gripe twice.

Response time is critical in dealing with complaints. The best time to address public concerns is "now." Procrastination is not an acceptable complaint-handling technique. No complaint should ever go unattended for more than twenty-four hours.

Even if no remedy is readily available, it is still better to face up to a complaint than to stonewall it. Saying something to an expression of dissatisfaction or displeasure is better than saying nothing. Sometimes, however, listening is all it takes to calm the complainant and restore confidence in the organization. Most people are usually patient, understanding, and forgiving as long as someone in authority is paying attention to their problem and, at least, looking for a solution.

The first rule for school personnel in handling complaints, then, is to act quickly and personally. You can't always solve every problem or satisfy every complainant, but you can always listen, and you can always try to find an answer—the sooner the better.

Naturally, not all wrongs can be rectified. The surprising thing about complaints, however, is that they don't have to be. As long as school personnel make an honest effort to help, most reasonable people will be satisfied. It's the "trying" that counts, not just the results.

Of course, saying or trying the wrong things can make matters worse. Insensitive or inappropriate responses can quickly turn a minor case of dissatisfaction into a major problem of public alienation. Below are twelve widely recognized don'ts for dealing with complaints about schools:

1. Don't hang up or refuse to accept complaints.

2. Don't fail to listen.

3. Don't become defensive.

4. Don't deny responsibility.

5. Don't bluff, give phony excuses, or blame others.

6. Don't belittle any complaint.

7. Don't try to confuse complainants with jargon or double-talk.

8. Don't get angry or combative.

9. Don't refuse to offer assistance.

10. Don't try to convince complainants that they have no legitimate gripe.

11. Don't patronize or talk down to complainants.

12. Don't offer only token remedies.

Knowing what to say when handling complaints is mostly a matter of attitude. If you accept it as an opportunity to help and a chance to demonstrate your diplomacy skills, you'll usually succeed in finding the right words for even the most difficult situations. The tips below can also boost your chances of satisfactorily resolving most complaints (see also the sample complaint response letter in Box 5.4):

- Always assume that the person has a bona fide complaint.
- Listen. Don't interrupt. Venting is part of the healing process for many people who believe they have been treated badly.
- Don't hurry. Let complainants tell their whole story.
- Probe for details. Be sure that all the facts are on the table.
- Don't be afraid to use pauses to indicate that you are thinking about the problem. Silences can provide mini cooling-off periods.
- Rephrase the complaint to verify understanding.
- Seek clarification if needed.
- Take notes. Don't count on memory to retain all details of each complaint.
- Accept blame when appropriate.
- Apologize even if you are not sure that you or the organization is at fault.
- Remain civil no matter how abusive the complainant becomes.
- Commit to looking into the issue.
- Give straight answers or get someone who can.
- Never promise what you can't deliver.
- If you can't personally satisfy the complainant, try to refer him or her to someone who can or lay out what options remain.
- Whatever you say, say it in a timely manner.

- Try to give the complainant some choices of remedies.
- Surprise everyone. Do a little more than the complainant expects.
- Follow up later to check on continued satisfaction. This is an added touch of class that too many school leaders overlook.

Box 5.4   Sample Complaint Response Letter

Dear_____:

Your concern about the new middle school math program has been brought to my attention. Please know that we take all such complaints seriously.

I sincerely apologize if there has been any misunderstanding or misinformation about this change in curriculum. We believe we have an improved way of helping students learn mathematics. The new program has been carefully researched and tested successfully in many school districts across the country. I hope your concerns are based on false data or reports. Let's find out.

I'd like to invite you to join me in visiting your child's math class and observing the program in action and/or to sit down with the chairman of our math department for a firsthand review of the program and the methods and materials being used in your child's class.

I'm sure we both want the best math education possible for our children. If there are problems with the new approach, I hope you will work with us to correct them.

Please call my office to make arrangements for us to reexamine the program together.

Thank you for sharing your concern. I look forward to meeting with you soon.

Sincerely,

_____
Superintendent of Schools

The suggestions above will help settle most cases of public dissatisfaction. Of course, some members of the public don't really want to be satisfied. They enjoy complaining too much. These people are chronic complainers. Every school district has a few. They can't or won't allow themselves to be satisfied. For these pathological complainers, "bitching" is a way of life and an end in itself. As Robert Kennedy once commented, "One-fifth of the people are against everything all the time."

As a school leader, you owe even these habitual complainers

- Reasonable attention and polite, active listening
- Honest answers
- A good-faith effort to solve any real problem

You don't owe them anything more. Dealing with an insatiable complainer shouldn't become your life's work. I'm reminded of a superintendent who grew tired of a habitual complainer who constantly demanded attention because "I help pay your salary." After he had enough, the superintendent calmly handed the pest a $1 bill and said, "Here's your share of my salary. Now, I don't want to hear any more of your complaints."

Don't waste an undue amount of time on chronic complainers. Listen to their complaints, help if you can, agree to disagree if you must, and move on.

Complaints are like bodily symptoms. They can tell you when something more serious is wrong or about to go wrong in your system.

A few complaints merely mean you're working with people. It goes with the territory. A lot of complaints, however, may signal some serious internal problems. No complaints may mean that your patrons are so turned off that they don't even bother to sound off anymore.

Dealing with disgruntled pupils, parents, and patrons is nobody's favorite pastime, but it is an essential function for school officials. Handling complaints is just another form of problem solving. As a principal or superintendent, that's what you are supposed to do best.

How to Make the Most of Good News

Thank God for good news! You've got to love it. But why include it as a topic in a book for school administrators on "how to say the right thing"? What can possibly go wrong telling the public good news? Nothing much—except it's a chance that shouldn't be slighted. It's too good an opportunity to mess up or pass up.

The whole world will make the most of any bad news involving your school district. But no one will make much of the good news that comes along—unless you do. It may not be a top priority, but it's worth some attention. Here are six points to ponder every time you have good news to share with the public:

1. Announce the news in clear, unmistakable terms. Make sure everyone "gets it." Use photos or videos if possible. (You know how much one picture is worth.)

2. Give specific credit to all who deserve it (and maybe a few who don't).

3. If the news involves kids, showcase them and their families in any announcement you make. Kids get attention. Be sure to let the parents share in the credit.

4. Refer to similar achievements or distinctions past and present. Point out the pattern. Let people realize that such incidents are not once-in-a-lifetime occurrences. They're just the way you do business.

5. Don't make the good news out to be more than it really is. But don't make it any less either. It doesn't pay to be smug, arrogant, or overly humble. Use appropriate descriptors or adjectives but don't go overboard. Too many superlatives can get tiresome and make you appear conceited, nerdy, desperate, or all of the above.

6. Be sure all the right people (i.e., teachers, parents, school board, legislature, etc.) hear the good news. It really isn't good news if no one hears about it.

Good news unreported is a missed opportunity. Don't let it happen on your watch.

When you say the right thing in the right way, you can make good news even better—and make it last longer. Why not get the biggest bang for your buck? It's one of the little secrets that separate true leaders from also-rans.

TRUTH IN TAXATION

I'm proud of paying taxes in the United Sates. The only thing is—I could be just as happy paying half the money.
—Arthur Godfrey

Be careful what you say to the public about taxes. Even presidents have been known to lose reelection bids for saying one thing ("Read my lips: No new taxes.") and doing another. There's a lesson here. Learn it.

Most people don't like taxes. They don't like to pay them. They think taxes are too high. They don't understand how taxes are calculated. Worst of all, they don't believe what public officials—including school leaders—tell them about taxes.

Obviously, this is a huge communication and credibility problem. If you want your community members to believe what you say about taxes and support the taxes your district proposes and imposes, it is absolutely essential that you tell the TRUTH (all of it) and make it UNDERSTANDABLE to laypeople every time, all the time. Anything less is unacceptable.

Don't even think about trying to mislead, misinform, or confuse the public concerning taxes. It will come back to bite you sooner or later without fail.

The average citizen's eyes glaze over whenever school business managers and other administrators start using technical tax terms such a property valuation, tax capital rate, certified levy, adjusted net tax capacity, or tax increment funding. Most people don't know what a mil is or understand the difference between a bond issue and an excess levy referendum.

Why should they? It's all jargon. Don't use it unless you clearly define each term, check frequently with your audience for understanding, and give lots of real-life examples.

The right thing to say to the public about taxes is always *the clearest, most honest statement you can make at the time.* Anything you can do to provide truth-in-taxation information in plain terms will go a long way toward making you a hometown hero (see Box 5.5).

Box 5.5 Sample Truth in Taxation

District Revenue Sources:

Local Taxes	49%
State Contribution	33%
Federal Contribution	3%
Other (Misc.)	15%

Total Levy (Tax) Comparison:

Payable 2007 General Fund	$24,193,005.86
Payable 2008 General Fund	$24,719,573.34

2008 Levy (Tax) Increase:

Gross Increase	$585,456.07
Percentage Increase	1.95%

School District Tax Impact for 2008:

Home Value	Amount of Tax Payable
$200,000	$1,901.76
$350,000	$3,643.98
$400,000	$4,233.36

Information provided by St. Louis Park (MN) Schools, December 2008.

With this in mind, following is the best advice you will probably ever get on what to say and how to talk to the public about taxes:

- Remember that taxpayers aren't cash cows. They're people. They are your neighbors. They pay your salary. They have certain rights (see Box 5.6). Respect them.
- Simplify all budget and tax information. Batch like items together. Use descriptive categories. Stick to common words.
- Provide real reasons for any tax increase or decrease.
- Use examples of the tax impact on real homes in your community.
- Break down the tax impact on a monthly, weekly, or daily level (e.g., 50¢ a day, less than the price of a cup of coffee).
- Compare your taxes with those of comparable school districts or other taxing agencies.
- Don't play games. Never refer to a reduced increase as a budget or tax "cut." Most people know better. The ones who don't are being conned. For most of us, a cut means the taxpayer actually pays less in total taxes tomorrow than they are paying today.
- Don't be afraid to play up the benefits of a tax increase. The public needs to know what their taxes are buying and to share in the pride of providing a good education for the youth of the community.

Box 5.6   Taxpayers' Bill of Rights

---

1. Right to a fair, equitable, reasonable, justifiable, and affordable tax bill.
2. Right to full and complete information concerning all taxes.
3. Right to plain English.
4. Right to know the basis of all tax increases.
5. Right to a one-on-one, sit-down review of individual tax bills.
6. Right to hardship relief when necessary.

Taxes are always a touchy topic. So always think before you talk about them, know what you're talking about, and be relentless in ensuring that everyone understands what you are saying.

Most people don't mind paying local taxes if they believe they are getting their money's worth. As a leader of the school, it's your job to show them that's what's happening. If it's not, then it's your job to start spending more wisely or to ask for lower taxes.

Of course, in today's educational economics, what is more likely to happen is that your taxes won't be enough and you'll end up asking for more money from other sources. But that's another whole section.

How to Ask for Money

If you are like most educators, you hate to ask for money. It seems unprofessional and demeaning. Get over it!

False pride is a luxury you (and all other school leaders) can no longer afford. Now more than ever before, school officials have to become "prospectors." The traditional tax-based school budget is now only one part of the funding support for schools.

Today, effective school leaders have to find, create, attract, or make extra sources of revenue to support their school programs. It's called survival. College presidents have been doing it for years. Now, it's your turn.

Whether it's seeking grants, soliciting funds for a school foundation, creating business partnerships, lobbying legislators for special funding, encouraging alumni contributions, or selling the community on passing an excess levy referendum, it's asking for money. It's what principals and superintendents do today.

It helps if you don't think of it as seeking charity (professional panhandling), asking for a handout, begging, or groveling. Instead, think of it as just another form of educating the public. There, that feels better already, doesn't it?

Unfortunately, many professional educators aren't very good at it. They're uncomfortable asking for money. They're too timid. They're embarrassed. They're too afraid of rejection. And if they don't change, they're obsolete.

When it comes to requesting money, success depends on trust and credibility. That requires being straight with people every day. Sound familiar?

If you really need money, the way to get it is to *just ask.* Don't hint. Don't float innuendos. Don't make vague suggestions. Don't expect people to guess. Don't rely on ESP. Ask straight out. Up front. Here's what it takes:

- Use positive language as much as possible. Talk about all the good the money will do, more than about all the bad things that will occur if you don't get it (see sample letter in Box 5.7).
- Don't downplay the negative consequences if more money isn't forthcoming (if schools are likely to be closed, the public needs to know). But don't exaggerate them either. Never cry "wolf" until the critter is actually at the door.
- Appeal to both the head and heart of potential contributors. Use hard data, but don't be afraid to throw in a few "chicken soup for the soul" anecdotes where appropriate.
- Explain the benefits of getting the money. Keep explaining until everyone "gets it."
- Establish the need. Be specific.
- Be absolutely truthful.
- Don't ask for more than you need.
- Avoid sermonizing. It's your job to make people feel good about giving, not guilty about not giving.
- Compare your costs and needs with comparable school districts and with state and national averages.
- Use hard-hitting words and phrases such as *crucial* or *worst-case scenario.*
- Keep any graphics simple.
- Convey a sense of urgency.

Box 5.7   Sample Fundraising Letter

Dear Fellow Citizen:

As you know, the school board is seeking public approval of a bond issue for $30 million to support new construction at our middle and senior high schools.

When successful, this referendum will allow us to give the children of the community state-of-the-art media centers, science labs, and technology centers. We hope you will join us in providing the best possible facilities for educating our children. The cost to you if you own a $200,000 home will be less than $10 a month.

The requested funds are needed because the two schools have not been remodeled, renovated, or refurbished in the last sixteen years. You know how much improvement your home would need after such a long period of neglect.

The amount being asked for in the referendum has been carefully pared down after lengthy discussions with local bankers, architects, and contractors. We are convinced this is a fair amount and a reasonable request. We hope you will agree.

Better schools mean a better community with higher home values. That's why we believe this referendum is a win-win situation for all age groups.

Please vote on Tuesday, November 11. If you have questions, feel free to contact any committee member at_____. Thanks for your support.

Sincerely,

_____
Citizens for Better Schools Committee

There are lots of ways to lead. One of them is to scrape and scrap for the resources to get the job done. You may think you don't like to ask for money, but you'll dislike not having enough even more.

You can do this. Let the real-world suggestions above help you find the right words to use in your unique situations. You'll be glad you did. So will your students.

"Houston, We Have a Problem": What to Say When Trouble Strikes

When trouble strikes or serious problems arise, the first, natural, instinctive response for most people is to protect themselves. That's why they often stutter, stammer, deny the problem, ignore it, downplay its seriousness, distance themselves, disclaim responsibility, claim ignorance, point fingers, bluff, stonewall, and even lie—"any port in a storm."

It's normal. It's natural. It's the easiest thing to say and do. It happens in schools as often as anywhere else.

But this isn't a book about how to say the easiest thing. It's about how to say the right thing in all school situations.

The best school leaders you know admit problems—even the nastiest, scariest, and most embarrassing ones—right away. Up front. So they can be faced. So they can be solved. So they can be forgotten.

The right time to own up to a problem to the public is as soon as possible. The right thing to say to the public about it is the truth. In the long run, it always pays to face problems head-on and out in the open. It's harder than ducking and running, but it's more responsible. It's the kind of leadership we call a "class act." It's the kind of leadership you want to provide for your community.

When crisis hits, the right things to say and do right away are

1. Become visible and immediately set the pattern of response for others to follow. Say SOMETHING as soon as possible. Be positive and candid. If it's a major crisis, one person should be designated as official spokesperson for the schools for the duration of the emergency.

2. Admit the problem. Define it. Explain what's happened without making excuses. Don't be defensive. Limit statements to facts. Avoid overexplaining or speculating. If it helps, use a prepared statement to avoid any impromptu ad libs that could prove embarrassing later on.

3. Briefly outline the alternative remedies available, being considered, or under way. If nothing else, say, "We're investigating."

4. Give your "refuse to panic" speech. Speak confidently about your efforts to resolve the problem. Reaffirm your commitment to making the safety of people and property a top priority.

5. Resist the urge to guess about how long resolution will take or how much it will cost.

6. Always promise to provide more full and complete information as soon as it is available. If possible, set a time for follow-up.

Later on, after the matter has been resolved, it helps to bring closure to the situation by

- Praising all those who helped eliminate the problem.
- Reinforcing how preparedness and quick action helped prevent the problem from being even worse than it was.
- Playing up the lessons learned and the preventive measures that have been put in place to avert a repetition of the problem.

The public forgets problems solved. It doesn't forget lies told or cowardly cover-ups. That's why, when trouble strikes, the best advice is to

- Stand up.
- Speak up.
- Take charge.

It's a leader's way.

How to Apologize and Admit Mistakes to the Public

Why is it so hard to say, "I'm sorry?" Offering an apology ranks right up there with accepting a compliment for most of us. It's one of the hardest things we ever have to do. And if you think apologizing to an individual is a challenge, try apologizing to the general public.

As public figures, most school leaders sooner or later have to apologize in public to the public for some mistake or shortcoming of the school. It's easier if you understand that public apologies are different. We've all seen politicians and other celebrities make apologies to the community. Some work. Some don't. What makes the difference?

The public requires that certain standards and conditions be met before an apology is deemed satisfactory. The public expects (a) a sincere admission of some specific fault, (b) full acceptance of responsibility, and (c) some sign of genuine remorse. Anything less is unacceptable.

When making a public apology, forget about weasel words, blame-shifting, excuse-making, or circuitous explanations. Keep it short. Keep it simple. And keep it straightforward. The anatomy of a successful public apology includes four features:

1. Regret

2. Remorse

3. Remedies

4. Restitution

The next time you make a mistake (and you will) and you have to apologize to your constituents or patrons, take this advice:

- Don't beat around the bush. Spit it out. Get on and get off quickly.
- Look 'em in the eye and admit the mistake right away. Take the blame. If it happened on your watch, it's your responsibility.

- Don't come across as reluctant, grudging, combative, or argumentative. An insincere apology is worse than no apology. Act as if you are anxious to make things right, not as if you are apologizing only because you got caught.
- Use the everyday words of apology (see Box 5.8).
- Dare to be humble. There is power in humility.
- Offer to make amends.
- Acknowledge lessons learned.
- Give assurances that it won't happen again.
- Where appropriate, apologize without admitting guilt by using statements that comfort but don't compromise your integrity, such as, "I'm sorry you feel that way" or "I'm sorry people are upset."
- Keep things in perspective. Don't blow the situation out of proportion, but don't downplay it either.
- Don't engage in apologetic overkill. Enough is enough. Once an apology has been made public, it doesn't need to be repeated over and over.
- Always apologize sooner rather than later. Putting it off only makes you appear guiltier.

Box 5.8   Terms of Apology

Accept	Forgive	Remiss
Admit	Forward	Responsibility
Amends	Future	Restitution
Apologize	Growth	Serious
Blame	Ill-advised	Shortsighted
Breach	Imperfect	Sorry
Concern	Mistake	Thoughtless
Correct	Omission	Unexpected
Disappoint	Opportunity	Unfortunate
Embarrass	Oversight	Unintentional
Excuse	Pardon	Violation
Failure	Rectify	Wrong
Fault	Red-faced	

An apology isn't an admission of weakness. It can be an act of courage and a sign of strength—an honest expression of sensitivity, compassion, empathy, and good conscience. Done properly, an apology can even gain you new respect.

Everyone has made mistakes. Everyone has had to apologize. Everyone knows how hard it is. That's why most people want to forgive and forget. Let them.

An apology isn't a big deal unless you make it one. Don't. When you make a mistake, admit it. When an apology is due, make it. Then move on. You have more important things to do than marinate in guilt or regret.

SPIN DOCTORING FOR AMATEURS

Some people hire other people to say the right thing for them. Politicians are known for employing spin doctors to put the best possible spin on things when they get into trouble or to help them explain their way out of scandal. Unfortunately, this is a luxury school personnel don't have.

As a school leader, you have to be your own spin doctor. But that's not a bad idea. Why not put the most favorable face on circumstances and events? Finding the proverbial silver lining helps balance the scale (put things into perspective), provide reassurance (it's going to be OK), restore confidence (we're on top of this), and start people thinking about solutions. These all sound like things a good leader should be doing anyway.

Of course, where some unscrupulous politicians and their damage-control artists may be willing to bend or rewrite the truth (see political survival spins in Box 5.9), school leaders have to stick to the facts. Luckily, you don't have to lie to find some good in most bad situations. Real spin doctoring isn't intended as a substitute for the truth. It's just telling or interpreting the truth in a different way (see sample spins in Box 5.10).

Spin doctoring is mostly a matter of attitude. Just think positive. All it takes is a sensitivity to the importance of perception, a commitment to optimism, and an eye for the overlooked.

The next time you have a setback and wonder what's the right thing to say, try a little spin doctoring. It works.

Box 5.9   Common Political Survival Spins

* It never happened.
* It's a conspiracy.
* It's not what it appears to be.
* It's not my fault.
* I haven't seen the report.
* Someone else did it.
* There's some mistake.

Box 5.10   Sample Spins for School Leaders

* It's a good thing it happened now rather than later.
* Fortunately, we were prepared. It gives us a chance to test our response capacity.
* It demonstrates our preparedness.
* It was a wake-up call.
* We're a stronger organization because of it.

DEALING WITH THE MEDIA: WHAT TO SAY TO REPORTERS

Talking to the media is different. When faced by a phalanx of reporters and/or an arsenal of microphones and TV cameras, you know this isn't an innocuous little conversation. This is news! It's scary, but sooner or later all school leaders have to do it.

When you talk to the media, what you say is going to be repeated and reported—not necessarily in the context it was given. And worse yet, hundreds—maybe thousands—of people will hear it or read about it. This is definitely the time to say the right thing.

Fortunately, it may not be as hard as you think it is. If you're nervous, it helps to remember that it won't take very long and that reporters are just people trying to earn a living. They are not out to get you or make you look stupid or foolish. You have to do that yourself.

You can handle reporters like a pro if you follow the tips below that media consultants routinely give to their clients:

- Answer all questions factually, without embellishment or editorializing. Tell reporters the truth. Tell them what you know. Don't engage in speculation, allegation, gossip, rumors, or guesswork.
- Be forthcoming with public information, but give opinions sparingly.
- Avoid jargon.
- Never lie to the media. (A colleague of mine learned this lesson the hard way when she closed school because of a bomb threat and told the media and the public it was because of a broken water main. Her intent was to avoid creating undue alarm. But when the truth surfaced (as it always does), members of the media were outraged and the administrator lost considerable credibility with the public. It was a well-meaning mistake, but a mistake nonetheless. It took a long time to earn back the trust lost because of one little white lie. Don't make the same mistake on your watch.)
- Get bad news over with quickly.
- Be careful about using or releasing names of pupils.
- If you don't know, say so.
- Never say, "No comment." It works on reporters like a red cape does on bulls.
- Adopt an up-front attitude. Don't come across as negative.
- Stay focused. Don't let reporters get you off track. Say what needs to be said regardless of what you are asked.

- Be concise. Today's media work with sound bites, not lengthy speeches.
- When necessary, divert questions by saying something like
  1. It would be premature to answer.
  2. That's a hypothetical question I can't answer at this time.
  3. I'm uncomfortable answering that until I know all the facts.
  4. I haven't seen the information yet.
- Always keep your promises to the media. Don't put reporters off. They have deadlines like everyone else.
- Never assume you are "off the record."
- Don't expect any favors from the press.
- Don't presume to tell reporters what is newsworthy.
- Think about your appearance. You're on TV. Look the part of a professional. It will add credibility to what you say.
- Look at the cameras and speak into the microphones. Don't back away.
- Keep your fingers crossed and hope the media don't find you on a slow news day.

If you are unaccustomed to it, speaking to the media may be nerve-racking. But knowing what to say to reporters is the easy part. Just tell them who, what, when, where, how, and why.

That's all they want to know. You can do this.

DO'S AND DON'TS OF PUBLIC SPEAKING FOR SCHOOL LEADERS

What's the worst part of communicating with the public for most school leaders? Giving a speech. Nothing else comes even close. There's something about public speaking that jellifies the joints and gives brave men and women podium paralysis.

Of course, this doesn't happen just to school leaders. Public speaking terrorizes leaders (and followers) in all fields. Most people fear speech giving almost as much as death itself.

But like it or not, some public speaking goes with the territory of being a school official. As a teacher, principal, or superintendent, you are required to speak at all kinds of conferences, conventions, convocations, commencements, and other community gatherings, large and small. To be a successful school leader today, you have to be able to say the right things in speech form.

There's no law, however, that says school leaders have to be golden-tongued orators. All they have to do is be able to deliver a clear message with feeling to groups of various sizes. Don't worry. It's doable with preparation, practice, and a few pointers from successful public speakers.

The first step is to make peace with the fear of facing an audience. It helps to realize that the anticipatory panic is almost always worse than the actual speaking experience itself.

In public speaking, delivery is as important as message. All of the preceding material can help you shape your message, while the do's and don'ts below can help sharpen your presentation skills.

So just take a deep breath, swallow hard, and follow these tips to deliver a knock-their-socks-off presentation every time.

Do's

- Do your homework. Take time to do all the preliminaries—researching, organizing, outlining, and preparing.
- Know your subject. Even when you know it well, it's still sometimes difficult to make your message clear. If you don't know what you're talking about, it's clear right away.
- Practice as much as necessary. Don't be afraid to rehearse your way to success.
- Check out the location of your speech in advance. Notice the seating, sight lines, acoustics, and lighting. Know how the mikes and sound system work and where the thermostat and light switches are.

- Use your nervous energy to be a more lively, animated speaker.
- Always have a goal and an audience in mind. Speak with a purpose and to a particular person.
- Look at the audience. Make eye contact with all segments of the room.
- Believe in your message. Give your own speech in your own words.
- Say what you mean. Be explicit. Watch out for ambiguities, mixed messages, or double meanings. Straight talk works equally well with groups as with individuals.
- Strive to start strong and end strong.
- Get to the point. Audience members shouldn't have to guess what the speech is about.
- Search for the simplest, clearest words. Choose words that both you and the audience are comfortable with. Remember that little words are better than big ones, and brevity rules.
- Get passionate. Enthusiasm begets enthusiasm. Let the audience catch some of yours.

Don'ts

- Adopt a phony persona. Don't act like a big shot speaker. Be yourself. Adopt a natural style and speak naturally.
- Ignore cultural differences in your audience. Err on the side of sensitivity and political correctness.
- Use emotionally charged words that might incite anger or bias.
- Overuse extraneous modifiers such as really, very, or totally.
- Insert too many adjectives—especially multisyllabic ones.
- Resort to sarcasm. It seldom works and often backfires.
- Put in a lot of technical gobbledygook.
- Rely on overused terms and phrases such as "awesome" and "you know."

- Tell jokes if you're not good at it. Especially refrain from using ethnic or risqué jokes. They may work at a comedy club, but not in a school auditorium.
- Dwell on negative topics or examples.
- Use lengthy, complicated, compound sentences. The audience isn't following along on a script. They can't see where you're going.
- Use flipcharts, overheads, PowerPoint charts, or other visual aids if you're uncomfortable with them.
- Run on too long. Know when to shut up. Your audience will love it.

The real secret to successful public speaking is to speak to an entire audience as if it were a single individual. Engage that one "person" with earnestness, sincerity, warmth, and good humor. Before you know it, everyone in attendance feels that you are talking personally and directly to them. It works every time. Now that the secret is out, you can forget about fear and have some fun giving speeches.

Whether it's an informal exchange with a few senior citizens or a major address to the chamber of commerce, you are the voice of the schools—the only voice some people ever hear. What you say can strengthen or diminish public perception of the school system. It's a big responsibility. Don't be paranoid, but take it seriously.

There's a reason we call them the "public schools." No public—no schools! When school leaders say the right things to get all of the public behind them, nothing can stop them. That's when everybody wins—especially kids.

6

How to Say the Right Thing in Special Situations

W ith repetition, handling most social situations becomes routine. But some never do. There are a few special occasions in which most people—even school leaders—feel clumsy, uncomfortable, awkward, and inadequate. For example, most of us have some trouble graciously accepting a simple compliment, pronouncing an invocation, saying "no" and making it stick, carrying on a conversation with a dying friend or colleague, comforting someone grieving the loss of a loved one, or giving a eulogy. We just never get used to these situations; and we always have difficulty finding the right words when these occasions arise.

As public figures, school officials are frequently involved in such situations more than most. Maybe that's why some people just assume you naturally know the right thing to say. If you don't, it's OK. There's nothing wrong with you. You're just mortal like the rest of us.

But help is available, if you want it, in the form of specific pointers for handling life's most awkward moments with, at least, a modicum of poise, grace, and dignity.

Anyone can learn to follow these tips. Most don't. You will be way ahead if you do. That's not a bad place for a leader to be.

Knowing what to say in awkward times can increase your "cool" and make you more confident and effective. More important, it will enable you to put others at ease and show them how to get through similar situations. That's another aspect of leadership they don't tell you about in Administration 101.

SECRETS OF SUCCESSFUL CEREMONIAL GREETINGS

No one has more large group meetings, events, functions, workshops, seminars, and convocations than school people. All of these gatherings require someone to deliver a brief ceremonial greeting (words of welcome). That someone is usually an administrator. (You know—you've been there, done that.)

If you are like many of your colleagues, you resent and resist performing this routine ceremonial function, because there's nothing new to say. And there's not enough time to say anything substantive or significant. Besides, nobody listens anyway. It's a meaningless ritual. It's just a perfunctory duty that takes more time than it's worth and wastes too much of your valuable time. Let someone else do it. (Am I getting close?)

For all these reasons, it's easy to blow off the assignment or not put any real effort into it. That's why you duck the duty if you can and just woodenly go through the motions if you can't.

Think again. You're missing the point. Giving a welcome or greeting isn't as trivial as you may think. As greeter, you set the tone for the entire event. Better yet, it's a perfect opportunity to make a positive impression on a lot of people in a minimal amount of time. That's an efficient use of time, not a waste of it.

If you can succeed in making those in attendance feel truly welcomed and good about being there, they will feel good about you and the schools you represent at the same time. Making a good impression is never a bad thing. Next time you're asked, relax and enjoy the opportunity to welcome a whole new audience.

What makes delivering greetings difficult for most of us is that everyone has heard it all before. How many ways are there to say, "You're welcome"? How can you say the right thing when it's already been said—countless times? Everyone usually knows what you are going to tell them before you even open your mouth. How can it be anything but boring?

The trick is to be sincere, keep it light, and make it seem fresh enough that the audience thinks they are hearing it for the first time. Here's how:

- Prepare. Think about what you want to say and how you want to say it. Even though it's going to take less than a minute or two, don't wing it. The shorter the message, the more thought it requires.
- Be sure to identify yourself. You can't make a good first impression or a lasting impression if people don't know who they are listening to.
- Show that you know who the audience is and what the event is about. Acknowledge the purpose of the gathering. Strive to make the greeting personal, not generic.
- Be upbeat and enthusiastic. Tell the audience why you are happy they are here and why you are glad to welcome them. If you use standard (stock) phrases such as "I'm glad you're here," "It's my pleasure," or "I want to welcome you on behalf of _____," say them like you mean them. Put some passion into them. Giving greetings to an audience is like pitching to a batter—it's all in the delivery.
- Give credit to the planners of the event.

- Don't say anything to downplay or trivialize the program. Respect and reflect the values and goals of the organization.
- Wish the audience well on the task at hand and urge them to have fun while at it.
- Offer your assistance in expediting the proceedings.
- Don't talk too long. When invited to give a "word of welcome," some speakers have done just that—stood up, said "welcome," and sat down. That may be a bit too terse. But shorter is better. A warm welcome can get a cold reception if it drags out too long.

There's not much different you can say when giving a greeting. What's new is that you have never said it to this particular audience on this specific occasion. Make the most of it.

Sometimes, the right thing to say is the same old thing—with renewed feeling. No one gets tired of hearing a compliment as long as it is sincere. The same thing is true of hearing welcoming comments at a meeting.

How to Give and Receive Compliments

What is it about compliments? Too many of us aren't sure when or how to give them and don't know the right thing to say to accept them graciously.

Nothing makes most people more uncomfortable, embarrassed, or self-conscious than receiving a compliment. Many people who are normally poised and controlled—you may be one of them—get totally tongue-tied or become all "aw-shucks" awkward when singled out for praise or a compliment. That's silly.

Educators, who make a living praising and complimenting kids, should know better. Fortunately, the fear of compliments is easily overcome. Anyone can learn to handle compliments. School leaders need to learn it to do their job.

The key to giving compliments is simplicity. Say what you feel. Nothing more. Nothing less. If you don't feel it, don't say it. Suit the praise to the situation. Don't gild the lily. Don't get all gushy. Don't be obscure either. Be honest, be direct, and be specific. Most people appreciate a quiet, sincere compliment but don't want a brass band.

Compliments are best received when they refer to some specific act, accomplishment, or trait. Generic compliments such as, "You're wonderful" often come across as phony. An insincere or phony compliment is worse than no compliment at all.

Timing is important too. The right time to give a compliment is immediately. As time goes by, even a well-intentioned compliment loses its impact.

Purists claim that a real compliment is always directed at the person, not at accessories. Instead of saying, "I love that dress," it's better to say, "You always know how to dress" or "You have a sense of style."

Likewise, they maintain that compliments should always refer to the receiver, not the giver. Don't say, "You always make me feel at home" or "I love your earrings." It's not about you or your feelings. It's about the other party.

That's what the purists say. In reality, any compliment is acceptable as long as it is sincere.

The biggest mistake people make when handing out compliments is to detract from their meaning by tying them to some caveat or qualifier. Don't express surprise that the person is or has done something worthy of a compliment. Don't couple a compliment with a veiled criticism (e.g., "You could do even better if you were on time more often."). Don't compare the person's success to some experience of your own. And don't link it to an expectation of even bigger successes in the future. People appreciate compliments but not added pressure.

A compliment is a gift. It should be freely given with no strings attached. Compliments mean the most when they stand alone.

Some people fear being too generous with their compliments. It can happen, but seldom does. Most adults are much more lavish with their criticism than with their praise. Take a tip from good teachers. Praise more and criticize less. You'll feel better. And so will the rest of the world.

If simplicity works in giving compliments, it works even better when accepting them. The worst thing you can do is protest when given a compliment. Trying to deny, reuse, reject, or deflect a compliment by claiming unworthiness is neither graceful nor gracious.

False modesty is phony. Nobody buys it. Trying to wiggle out of a compliment is an insult to the person complimenting you. If you don't think you deserve the praise, why should anyone else.

No matter how complicated we try to make it, accepting a compliment should be easy. All you have to know is the one surefire, foolproof, 100% guaranteed way to graciously accept any compliment, anytime, anywhere:

Just say—THANK YOU!

That's all it takes. You can't improve on it. If you want or need more, however, you can always

- Acknowledge the contributions of others.
- Express how the compliment makes you feel (e.g., happy, surprised, thrilled, excited).
- Be modestly modest, but not ungrateful.
- Add phrases such as "I'm glad you feel that way" or "Your support means a lot."

But a simple "thank you" will always suffice. Count on it.

The right thing to do with compliments is give them freely whenever you honestly feel they are deserved. The right thing to say when complimenting or being complimented is whatever is honest and heartfelt. It's a short lesson. Learn it now. Too many people never do.

How to Show Appreciation and Say "Thank You"

How hard can it be to say two words? You would be surprised. More people than you might ever imagine have difficulty saying a simple "thank you" convincingly. If it's bizarre that lots of people choke on a compliment, it's even stranger that a sincere "thank you" sticks in so many throats. The only reason for conveying thanks is to get another party to fully appreciate how deeply you appreciate their act or gift. This is a particularly important message for school leaders to get across to students, staff, parents, volunteers, lawmakers, taxpayers, and others. If you can't convince these groups that you are credible, believable, and sincere in appreciating their support, you might lose it.

Showing appreciation should be easy. And it is—if you don't screw it up by over-embellishing or trying to be cute. Just as in accepting a compliment, simplicity and sincerity are all that matters.

You just can't do any better than a plain "thank you very much" to show appreciation. If you want to spice it up, it's OK to tack on the following:

- Say something about the giver as well as the gift.
- Spell out precisely what you appreciate most about the gift or deed.
- Comment on how the act or gift was just right for you.

Add a dash of enthusiasm. That's all. Don't do any more. It works every time. Good leaders quit while they're ahead.

HOW TO SAY "NO" AND MAKE IT STICK

Don't be afraid to say no. . . . You can't manage your time if you give it to everyone who asks for it.

—Mary Kay Ash

As indicated earlier, lots of people have trouble accepting a simple compliment. Some even have difficulty saying thank you. But the hardest word in the English language for many to say is "no."

School leaders have as much or more trouble than most. It's unfortunate, because, properly used, "no" can be a leader's best friend and ally.

The word "no" gets a bum rap in our society. Too many people think of it strictly as a negative response to be avoided whenever possible. From childhood on, most of us have been conditioned to comply—to say "yes." That's why many adults actually feel guilty saying "no." They're wrong. "No" is a tool. Putting it to work is just another way to set priorities.

Saying "no" can save your time and your sanity. It's usually worthwhile to remain open (say "yes") to life—new ideas, opportunities, challenges, and experiences. But it's also important to recognize and respect the power of "no." Using it can change your life forever.

Of course, it doesn't work if you don't mean it or if you equivocate or qualify it. The word "no" shouldn't mean maybe (see waffle words and phrases in Box 6.1).

If you want others to really believe you and respect your decision, here's the right way to say "no" and make it stick:

- Develop your own inner standard for when to say "no."
- Decide in advance how tough you are willing to be to stick with "no."
- Don't hint or imply. Speak with conviction. Be firm, clear, and direct. There's a reason why you see the words, "What part of 'no' don't you understand?" on the office wall in some schools.
- If appropriate, explain your reason(s) for having to decline, but stay away from lengthy explanations or excuses. Keep it short.
- Ignore any urge to lie to get off the hook. Tell the truth even if it's touchy. Lies tend to be discovered and discovery tends to be embarrassing.
- State regret at having to decline.
- Try to say "no" in a nice way. Decline in a positive manner. Pay a compliment as you decline if possible. ("Phrasing a negative response in a positive way

allows you to maintain relationships, foster friendships, and avoid hurt feelings." —Victor M. Parachin)

- If the request was in writing, respond in writing. You
never know when a paper trail will come in handy
later on.
- Don't leave the door open for negotiation, reconsid-
eration, argument, nagging, or second-guessing.
Instead, stay relaxed and be ready to repeat your
refusal as often as it takes.

Box 6.1   Waffle Words and Phrases

Maybe	Not certain	Don't know
Perhaps	Probably	May not
Unsure	Don't think so	I guess

Don't go overboard and start saying "no" to everything.
Like any tool, the word "no" can be overused.

Saying "no" takes guts. Saying "yes" doesn't take anything. When you value yourself enough to say "no," you can
finally gain control of your time, your job, and your life.

As the head of your organization, you will earn more
respect by saying "no" than by letting everyone down (including yourself) because you've taken on too much. There's a difference between a negative obstructionist and a patsy. Effective
school leaders don't want to be either. The trick is to know
when to say "go" and when to say "no."

When it's the right choice, saying "no" feels good. Try it.
Make it a part of your everyday vocabulary on the job.
Sometimes, "no" is the only right thing to say.

TIPS ON TESTIFYING

There is one special situation to which school leaders can't say
"no." In today's litigious society, school officials are frequently

called on to testify in court or in other, quasi-legal proceedings. These are not invitations you can refuse.

If there is one time when you want to be sure to say the right thing, it's when you are under oath. It's not always as easy as it looks, but if you stick to the following standard guidelines, you can't go wrong:

1. Allow yourself to be coached by legal counsel. That's what they are for.

2. Prepare thoroughly. Review all the facts, records, and evidence available. Know what you are talking about. It keeps you from being intimidated.

3. Dress and act like a professional. It adds to your credibility as a witness.

4. Listen carefully to all questions and to all instructions from the presiding judge or other authority. Don't be afraid to ask for clarity.

5. Take your time. Stay focused. Think before you speak.

6. Tell the truth, but not necessarily everything you know. Answer only what is asked. Answer yes and no questions with one word. Don't embellish, elaborate, or offer extraneous information. This isn't a suggestion. It's a rule.

7. Keep answers as short as possible. Stifle the urge to keep adding details.

8. Remain confident. Nobody knows what you know better than you do. Speak with certainty. It goes a long way in making your testimony believable.

9. Don't theorize, guess, grandstand, bluff, or lie. If you're not sure, say so.

10. It's OK to appear nervous. That's natural. But act forthcoming, not reluctant, reticent, or belligerent. Don't argue.

11. Look to your counsel for cues when needed.

12. Remain calm. Stay controlled. Any emotional outburst or demonstration of "attitude" will not help your testimony and may get you a contempt charge.

Testifying usually isn't fun, but it is always interesting. Just remember to remain guarded to ensure that your testimony is choreographed, not manipulated.

ADVICE FOR LEADING PRAYERS, GIVING INVOCATIONS, AND PRONOUNCING BENEDICTIONS

We live in a nation committed to the principle of separation of church and state. Religious prayers, invocations, and benedictions aren't supposed to play a role in public school functions. It may be controversial, but it's a fact of life in America.

Nevertheless, these religious practices do creep into school-sponsored events, activities, and ceremonies. In some parts of the country, they are the norm.

If, along with baccalaureate ceremonies, the practice of prayer or giving invocations and benedictions is traditional and acceptable to the community, it may be only a minor concern or a nonproblem altogether. But if school leaders are expected to engage in such activities, it can be tricky. What is the right thing for a public school principal or superintendent to say when leading a prayer, giving an invocation, or pronouncing a benediction at a school event?

In addition to the separation issue, there is always the issue of diversity. What is appropriate for a mixed gathering representing many faiths or denominations?

The best advice for school leaders is to leave praying to preachers and rabbis. If at all possible, it's wise to decline or avoid playing any religious role while serving as a secular leader in the community. But if you can't get out of it, the following suggestions will probably get you through the experience without stirring up any controversy or offending any individuals or groups.

- Tailor your remarks to the audience. (Is it primarily one faith or diverse? Is it mostly secular or mostly religious?)
- Use ecumenical terms and phrases. Consider using such references as Eternal Spirit, rather than God or Jesus.
- Strive to be broadly inspirational rather than narrowly religious. Inspirational quotations are always safe.
- If you must pray, stick to conventional prayers. Pray for peace, strength, or wisdom. Pray for the poor and needy. Bless the children. These are always safe topics.
- Avoid humor.
- Be low-key.
- Be brief (30–60 seconds is usually enough).

When a school leader is called on to perform some religious function in a school situation, the goal should be to avoid creating a problem where none exists. Keep the peace. God (and the school board) would want it that way.

WHAT TO SAY TO SOMEONE WHO IS NOT GOING TO GET WELL

The special situations covered in the preceding pages pose real communication challenges for many people, but those outlined in the remainder of the chapter pose huge communication problems for EVERYONE! They deal with issues of death and dying, such as what to say to a terminally ill patient.

These are real life's most serious and personal situations when people naturally look to leaders as models and count on persons in authority to help them deal with the emotions involved. These are tests of leadership that most of us would prefer to avoid, but some opportunities are not optional.

One of the most humbling experiences any of us ever has is searching for the right words to use with someone who is terminally ill. We've all had friends or co-workers who were not going to get well. We've all agonized over what to say to them.

Part of the problem is fear—not the dying person's, but our own. Since most of us have not faced imminent mortality, we don't know how it feels and we don't know where to begin, what to talk about, or what to say.

When communication with a terminally ill person is difficult or awkward, it's usually not the sick person's problem. It's ours. It's mostly a matter of our attitude. It often helps to think of the other person not as someone who is dying, but as the friend or co-worker we have known all along.

Dying people are still people. Different. Diverse. Varied. The first step in relating to those who are terminally ill is to accept them as the individual they are first and as a terminally ill person second.

As Reni Lang of the Stanford (Connecticut) Health System advises, "Accept and understand whatever reaction the patient has. . . . There's no one way to be a dying person. It's OK for the patient to be however she is."

Most people who are dying know it and go through the same classic stages of grief that their loved ones experience after they are deceased, including:

- Denial
- Anger
- Bargaining
- Depression
- Acceptance

Everyone progresses through the steps at their own pace and not necessarily in any particular order. Authentic conversation is facilitated by recognizing what step the person is on.

Don't assume that all dying people are depressed. Some accept—even welcome—their own mortality.

It's always difficult to know what to say when confronted with death, but not saying anything or avoiding someone you know who is dying is not a grown-up alternative. Terminally ill people are comforted by human company. Period. Have you ever heard anyone say, "I want to die all alone, separated, and isolated from all those I know and love"?

When you have a friend or colleague who is not going to get well, you have a duty as a friend, as a fellow human being, and as a leader to offer your comfort and your company. If you don't have all the right words, silence—even a long silence—is OK.

But you can do better than silence. You can overcome the awkwardness. Professionals who work daily with death and dying know what helps and hinders meaningful dialogue with someone who is dying. Take their advice below. You'll be glad you did.

- Let the dying person steer the conversation and set the pace. No topic is taboo. It's OK for a terminal patient to question or challenge treatment options.
- Remember that terminally ill people are naturally self-absorbed. Give them slack. Forgive their self-indulgence.
- Don't talk like a minister or chaplain. Talk like a regular person. Go light on euphemisms. Dare to use the words *death* and *dying*.
- Accept the person's views and beliefs about spirituality. This is no time to attempt conversion.
- Don't try to "fix" the person's outlook. Just listen and empathize.
- Let dying individuals make plans and decisions as long as they want to and can. Allow them to tackle unfinished business. If the person wants to make funeral plans, don't try to stop it. Just ask how you can help.

- Don't contradict or argue with someone who is terminally ill. Likewise, don't deny reality. This is not the time to play Pollyanna. Don't suggest that the person is going to get well when you both know it's not going to happen. Straight talk works even at the end.
- When appropriate, get physically close to the person. Talk at eye level. Keep in mind that sometimes a touch is the right thing to say.
- Join the person in relishing happy memories. Laughter is OK.
- Help the person to feel good about the life he or she has lived.
- Say your goodbyes. Just having the opportunity to say them is a gift for both of you.

It's hard to know what to say to a friend or colleague who is terminally ill. It's even harder not to try. It's the trying that counts. Everything else is a plus. Following the commonsense advice above will multiply your pluses.

How to Express Sympathy

Knowing what to say to someone who is dying is difficult. Knowing what to say to their survivors after they die isn't any easier. Sympathy is easy to feel but hard to express.

Death happens. Schools are not exempt. Students die. Staff members die. Family members of employees die. In all these situations, people expect the school leader to lead the way in reaching out and expressing sympathy to the grieving survivors. It's part of the bargain of being a leader.

Finding the right words to say to mourners and survivors starts by appreciating what they are going through. Psychologists call it empathizing, which simply means projecting your personality into theirs to gain better understanding of their current feelings. It's trying to see the world through their eyes.

It helps to understand that grieving is hard work. In addition to the classic phases of grieving mentioned earlier, the process includes:

1. Accepting reality

2. Experiencing the pain

3. Adjusting to a new environment without the deceased

4. Finding a way to memorialize the loved one who died

Expressing sympathy doesn't have to be complicated. The best advice is to keep it simple and sincere and to avoid sermonizing. Saying something clumsy or indelicate is better than saying nothing. Avoidance feels like abandonment to a survivor. If you can't do anything else, just listen and hug. The message will still get through.

Although words may be difficult to come by and may seem inadequate to express deep emotions, they are the best tools we have. Think about what to say in advance. The words you choose and how you use them make a difference.

It helps to say:
- I'm sorry.
- I want to help.
- Our thoughts and prayers are with you.
- I'm here if you need me.
- I have good memories of him.
- I don't know what to say.
- We will miss her.
- You have lots of friends who care about you.
- Let me do this much for you.
- I'll never forget the time _____.
- It's OK to cry. We all did.

It doesn't help to say:
- It was God's will.
- Time heals all wounds.
- I hope I die like that.

- He's not suffering anymore.
- It's probably for the best.
- I know how you feel.
- You'll get over it.
- It was a good way to go.
- You must get hold of yourself.
- At least you have the kids.
- It's better this way.
- You're still young.
- Chin up.
- Don't cry.
- She looked so lifelike.

Whatever you say, don't worry about making the survivors feel bad. They already feel that way. If you ask them, "How are you doing?" expect them to say "OK." Also expect them not to mean it.

Never assume that survivors don't want to talk about the deceased. They do. Let them. Give them permission to say whatever they are feeling. There is no way that a third party can talk them out of their pain, but letting them talk speeds the healing process.

There are many other ways to offer meaningful sympathy and support. Most authors in the field recommend the following:

- Say something personal about the deceased.
- Don't be afraid to speak the deceased's name; resist the urge to hide behind euphemisms (e.g., passed away, passed on, departed, etc.). The person is dead. Everyone knows it. Say the words out loud. The more they are spoken, the easier it is to deal with the accompanying emotions.
- Don't feel you have to whisper. Speak naturally. You're not going to wake the dead.
- Choose your words from the conventional vocabulary of grieving (see Box 6.2). Many of the terms are code words of comfort.
- Use lots of "remember whens."

Box 6.2   The Language of Grieving

Admiration	Goals	Peace
Affection	Good	Prayers
Affirm	Good times	Recollections
Alone	Grief	Redemption
Beloved	Happier times	Religious
Bereavement	Happiness	Remember
Blessed	Hasn't sunk in	Renewal
Brave	Healing	Resilience
Burial	Healthy	Respect
Busy	Heartfelt	Reverence
Celebrate	Heaven	Reviewal
Cemetery	Help	Richness
Children	Heritage	Sadness
Church	History	Saintly
Comfort	Hope	Service
Condolences	Inheritance	Shared
Courage	Interment	Shrine
Cremation	Joy	Sincere
Crying	Kindness	Solace
Death	Lasting	Sorrow
Deceased	Legacy	Spirit
Depression	Life	Suffering
Deserved	Lonely	Support
Devoted	Loss	Survive
Difficult	Loved	Sympathy
Emotions	Many friends	Tears
Empathy	Marriage	Thoughts
Eulogy	Martyr	Time
Example	Memorial	Timeless
Faith	Memories	Together
Family	Misery	Tough
Feelings	Missed	Treasure
Fondness	Mourning	Understanding
Forever	Neighbors	Unexpected
Forgiving	Not alone	Unforgotten
Friends	Numb	Values
Funeral	Ordeal	Vulnerable
Future	Pain	Wake
Generous	Partner	Worship
Gift	Patience	

- Emphasize good memories. It's OK to laugh.
- Stress how important the deceased was to other people. Talk about what will be most remembered about the person.
- Pay tribute and honor the deceased's contributions.
- Don't get overly religious or preachy. Too much piety can come across as both phony and patronizing. This is no time to proselytize.
- Offer specific help, not cheap advice.
- Don't dwell too much on your feelings or emotions. You're supposed to be the sympathizer, not the sympathizee.
- Avoid overly dramatic references, such as "tragic" or "appalling."
- Don't rely on worn-out platitudes.
- Avoid the worst faux pas of all—asking for something that belonged to the person who just died. Sound gross? It happens. If you need convincing, read Lynn Kelly's *Don't Ask for the Dead Man's Golf Clubs* (2000).
- Don't cross the line between sympathy and pity. Sympathy is supportive. Pity is patronizing.
- Keep your remarks brief. Don't monopolize the mourner. Others want to convey their condolences too.
- For an extra touch of class, make your sympathy more than a one-stop event. Remember the survivors later at holiday time and especially on the anniversary of the person's death. Your remembering won't be forgotten.

As leader of the schools, you are perceived as the voice and heart of the system. That's why it is doubly important for you to reach out to show sympathy when one of your own dies or loses a loved one.

If for some reason you cannot convey your sympathy in person, send a personalized, handwritten note. If even that is impossible, let Hallmark do it. Just do it. Don't put it off. Don't forget about it.

Expressing sympathy isn't just something nice for you to do. It is something you have to do to demonstrate how people in the organization are supposed to treat each other. Besides, it's the right thing to do.

HOW TO GIVE A EULOGY

No one feels fully adequate to deliver a eulogy. Who can honestly pretend to do justice to the task? How can anyone find the right words to pay sufficient tribute or satisfactorily summarize another human being's life? But someone has to do it. Often, it's the leader of the organization.

As a teacher, principal, or superintendent, sooner or later you will probably be called on to eulogize a former student, co-worker, or employee. It's an awesome responsibility. It's also an honor—one you can't hide from. Awesome or not, just try. You can do this. If you doubt it, read on.

The secret is to set realistic expectations for your "performance." Don't feel that you have to speak only words worthy of being carved in stone. You don't. Others don't expect it.

One of the things that makes delivering a eulogy doable is that you are speaking to a friendly, receptive, and understanding audience. People understand the delicacy and difficulty of the task. They realize that you are speaking for all mourners and will be pulling for you to succeed. They are glad that you are doing it instead of them. They don't expect miracles. Why should you? There is only one rule: Do your best.

It helps to understand what a good eulogy is. The word *eulogy* comes from Latin and Greek roots and roughly means "praise." The whole point is simply to praise the deceased and affirm that his or her life was worth living. A good eulogy is a celebration of who the deceased was. There are only three requirements for an effective eulogy:

1. Speak from the heart.

2. Emphasize good experiences and memories.

3. Speak no ill of the deceased.

As with all special situations, there are a few promptings that can make it more manageable and help you say the right thing. Here they are:

- Don't try to talk like a minister. Be yourself. Speak naturally—like a friend.
- Aim your remarks toward the specific audience. (Are they mostly family? Co-workers? Friends?)
- State your purpose. "We're here to honor and remember _____."
- Define your relationship with the deceased. Don't feign intimacy that didn't really exist.
- Refer to the common bond uniting the mourners.
- Be respectful, but don't deify the deceased.
- Share a memory or personal experience with the person who died.
- Tell a funny story involving the deceased.
- Tell why you (and others) like the deceased.
- Tell why the person will be remembered.
- Tell what you will celebrate most about the deceased's life.
- Stress the value of the deceased's contributions and accomplishments.
- Acknowledge your feelings of loss. Emphasize why you will miss the person.
- Suggest how the audience can help memorialize the deceased.
- If you have to pause to compose yourself, don't worry about it. The audience will empathize. They may need to collect themselves as well. Just gulp and go on.
- If you are comfortable with it, speaking directly to the deceased can be effective.
- Consider closing with the deceased's favorite quote(s) or poem(s), if appropriate.

A eulogy is the most important speech the deceased will never hear. It deserves your best effort. But that's enough.

Once it's done, don't agonize over it. You should feel good about accepting the challenge.

People probably won't remember exactly what you said. They will remember that you did what needed to be done to honor a friend and colleague. That's what leaders do.

Many of the special situations in this chapter don't happen very often. Their importance, however, is disproportionate to their frequency.

Let the chapter be a wake-up call to remind you that what school leaders say in any situation may turn out to be significant. People notice what you say and remember even off-the-cuff remarks. The lesson is that all the time is the best time to try to say the right thing. Public officials are always in somebody's spotlight.

If you can't live with that, then the right thing to say is, "I quit."

7

How to Say the Right Thing in Writing

I see but one rule: to be clear.

— Stendhal

About half of the population think they are capable of writing the great American novel. The other half think they are incapable of writing anything and are afraid to even try. As a school leader, if you are in the second category, you've got a problem.

Leaders in all fields have to write. That means you have to write. It's part of the job. Writing is something most administrators do every day. History says that Napoleon wrote 50,000 letters in his lifetime. That sounds like an average week to many principals and superintendents.

Unfortunately, some school leaders muddle through their entire careers and never get any better at writing memos, reports, recommendations, proposals, plans, articles, columns, critiques, business letters, personal notes, or even e-mail messages. It's usually their fault. They don't try.

You can do better. If you really want to say the right thing in writing, dare to diagnose what you write. The key to improvement is simply to know your weak spots and work on them. Become your own worst critic. Take a hard look at what you're doing right and what you're doing wrong. Ask for feedback from someone you trust. (How about one of your English teachers?) Take your time rewriting. Improvement is guaranteed.

What's hard about writing is that it is never perfect—it can always get better. What's easy about writing is that the fundamentals are attainable. You can become an effective writer. Anyone can. Practice helps. So does an understanding of the symbiotic relationship between speaking and writing.

WRITING IS DIFFERENT—OR IS IT?

Every day, school leaders communicate in writing to students, staff, parents, the public, and/or the media. Nevertheless, writing still scares many teachers, principals, and superintendents.

Most educators are reasonably comfortable with their ability to communicate orally, but many freeze up at the prospect of writing. It's not uncommon for school personnel to believe that anyone can talk, but that it takes someone who is a Hemingway or better to write well. They're wrong!

Writing doesn't have to be fancy, poetic, formal, complicated, or eloquent. In fact, it shouldn't be if you want to get your point across to busy, ordinary people.

When school leaders develop written materials, the overriding goal should be simply to produce copy that is easy to read and easy to grasp. If what you write is hard to follow or understand, it will never get read. So much for communication.

The best way for educators to write for any audience is the same way they would speak to the same audience. The closer your writing is to your everyday conversational style, the more likely it is to be accepted and understood.

What works for effective speaking (i.e., plain words, simple statements, specific examples, and lots of action verbs) works for writing as well. Whether it's drafting a memo, a report, a note to a student, a letter to parents, a recommendation, or a reprimand, the same rules apply.

It's amazing that more people don't grasp the simple principle of writing like you speak. If you are like many people, you may think that when you write, you should sound like an "author." You shouldn't. You should sound like yourself. (Of course, you might want to omit some of the ums, ahs, and "you knows" that clutter up everyday speech.)

Try reading what you write out loud. If it sounds like you normally speak, it's OK. It will get your message across. If it sounds stiff, stuffy, and stilted, it's not going to work.

Effective school leaders refuse to be scared off by a simple pen, pencil, or keyboard. No matter if you are speaking or writing, the words all come from the same place. Choosing the right thing to write works the same way as choosing the right thing to say. In one sense, writing is easier than speaking, because you can polish what you say before it touches anyone.

Like speaking, writing is just putting one word after another. The secret is to be sure you use honest, clear, and understandable words. Good writing isn't mysterious; it's just straight talk on paper. As it turns out, then, writing isn't so different after all.

A No-Nonsense Writing Clinic
for School Leaders

It is common knowledge among managers that the written word often communicates a stronger message than the spoken word.
                                                                —Unknown

If you can say it, you can write it. It's that simple. There is no reason that you (or anyone) can't learn to write effectively in and for every school situation—if you are willing to pay attention and practice.

Don't make the common mistake of thinking that writing can be set in motion only by some ethereal muse or, at least, by some flash of inspiration. Inspiration is rare. It's a luxury. And there aren't enough luxuries to go around. Don't wait for the right mood or muse to strike you. There's writing to be done. Do it.

Of course, writing is work; but it can also be fun because it is creative. Words are pieces of a puzzle. Writing is merely finding the right pieces and putting them in place to create a complete picture. If you like puzzles, you can enjoy the challenge of writing.

To become an effective writer, write. That's what the best principals and superintendents do. They accept writing as part of the job, do it to the best of their ability (which keeps getting better), and have some fun in the process.

The advice that follows isn't intended as a graduate course in "Advanced Expository Writing Techniques"—rather, it consists of some commonsense, basic, roll-up-your-sleeves rules for everyday writing. If you stick to them, you will get the job done. Your writing may not be lyrical or poetic or deathless prose, but it will be readable, understandable, and believable. That's all you need to achieve in your writing as a school official.

The pointers below are the best advice you will probably ever get on writing; amazingly, they are all you will ever need to know to succeed. But they work only if you apply them. Apply them, starting now:

- The first rule (maybe the only really necessary rule) is "write to express, not impress" (—Bob Bly). Writing is for communicating, not showing off. Be clear. Be absolutely understandable. Make it impossible for any reader to miss the point. Sound easy? It's not. But it is the standard for good writing as a professional educator.

- Find the right place to write. It may not be your office. Some writers work best at a stand-up desk. At least one can only write using a lapboard while sitting on a favorite couch. Whatever works.

- Always write for a reason, not just to prove that you are busy, important, or powerful. Writing without a goal is drivel.

- Have a specific audience (person or group) in mind when you write. ("When I write, I aim in my mind not toward New York but a vague spot a little east of Kansas." —John Updike)

- Do all the preliminaries (i.e., planning, researching, organizing). Prewriting is as important as rewriting.
  1. Do your homework. Know what you are writing about. You owe your readers that much.
  2. Think before you write. Pin down your thoughts. Decide in advance what to include in and what to include out. Good writing is focused, not random.
  3. Take time to outline (mentally or on paper) all your written work. An outline is a blueprint for successful writing.

- Follow the steps most professional writers use (Box 7.1).

- Strive to write logically. Arrange your points in order. If you write in a logical sequence, readers won't get lost.

- Writing is mostly a matter of making choices. Make good ones. Choose your words carefully. Take time to consider alternatives. Pick out the best and write one word at a time.

Box 7.1   Steps in Effective Writing

---

1. Plan.
2. Outline.
3. Rough draft.
4. Set aside. (Good writing needs to marinate.)
5. Proofread (twice).
6. Polish (finishing touches).

- When possible, opt for the short word, sentence, and paragraph. Avoid run-on sentences. (Try to limit sentences to seventeen words or less.) Break long strings of words into manageable lengths. We live in a sound-bite society. Readers are busy and in a hurry. They have short attention spans. Get in, get your point across, and get out quickly and you will never lose a reader.
- Don't use jargon (technical or professional terms) or legalese unless you absolutely have to.
- Omit useless words. Distrust too many adjectives. And be adverse to the overuse of adverbs.
- Start general and work your way toward specifics.
- Vary sentence length and construction to heighten interest.
- Think about how your writing sounds to the reader (tone). Is it patronizing? Bossy? Whiny? Intimidating?
- Give as much time and effort to writing for students as to writing for peers, parents, or other adults. ("You write for children the same way you write for grown-ups—only better." —Maxim Gorky)
- Pay attention to grammar. Bad grammar produces bad sentences; but avoid "grammar phobia." Don't be so slavish to rules that your writing sounds phony. Writing that is too perfect is boring.
- Be conscious of appearance. Leave lots of white space. It makes the page look more friendly and inviting.

- Don't quit too soon. Some rewriting almost always helps. Consider Stephen King's formula for rewriting: Second draft = first draft minus ten percent.
- Avoid overkill. Readers can get buried by too much detail. Remember, you are not being paid by the word.
- If you are unsure or under extreme time pressure, dare to use form letters or borrow from collections of sample letters, memos, or speeches (see References, Resource C). When you are lame, it simply makes sense to use a crutch.
- Lighten up and enjoy your writing. Celebrate (reward yourself) when you are done.

The suggestions above are worth rereading. They work. Try them. You'll be glad you did, because, like it or not, some writing skill is essential to success as a school leader.

Fortunately, there is no magic about good writing. ("There are no secrets. There are only words and your ability to arrange them." —Michael Perry) You can do this.

Becoming a great writer isn't going to happen to most of us. To be good enough, however, is within everyone's grasp. All it takes is following the tips above every time you tackle a new writing assignment—whether it's preparing a major formal report or drafting a routine memo.

INTEROFFICE MEMOS:
THE GOOD, THE BAD, AND THE UGLY

Anyone can write a memo. Not everyone, however, can write a memo that motivates readers, triggers action, and gets results.
—Robert Ramsey

God must love memos. He makes so many of them. Memos are everywhere. They are the paper trail of all organizations, especially schools. Everybody writes them. Everybody gets them. Some even read them.

Good memos stand alone and answer questions before they are asked. Bad memos confuse the situation. Ugly memos make things even worse.

Obviously, memos are used for a variety of purposes. The best ones

- Clarify goals, issues, or problems.
- Present new information.
- Define responsibility.
- Pinpoint accountability.
- Settle disputes.
- Outline proposals, plans, or recommendations.
- Lay out arguments.
- Persuade readers.
- Establish a record.

The scary thing about memos is that people can keep them. What you write can come back to haunt you. That should change the way you think about the lowly memo.

Don't underestimate their importance. Memos are a necessary part of doing business as a school leader. It pays to do them right. It's not that hard. Just keep these points in mind and you can't go wrong:

- Never write a memo when you have nothing to say or when another communication tool will work better.
- Think before you write. Careless thinking and sloppy memos go hand in hand. Keep in mind that some people will judge you by the memos you write.
- Make sure that readers learn something new from your memos. Otherwise, they are just exercises in repetition.
- Remember: Short memos get read. All others only get skimmed, filed, or tossed.
- If possible, limit each memo to a single topic. A good memo illuminates like a laser beam, not a floodlight.
- Be as concise as possible. Say what you mean. Say it clearly. Say it quickly. And stop. It's that "straight talk" thing all over again.

- A memo is a business communication, not a friendly letter. Get to the point quickly. Make your purpose clear right away. Readers shouldn't have to guess what a memo is about. Put the bottom line (goal or conclusion) first.
- Favor simple words. Avoid pretentious language (e.g., try substituting *start* for *commence*).
- Keep your memos lean and mean. Eliminate all useless words.
- Use the active voice and lots of action words.
- Keep sentences and paragraphs short. Limit each sentence to no more than two lines.
- Number items in a series.
- Use bullets to highlight important points.
- Always make clear what is expected of the reader.
- If appropriate, include a deadline for responding.

A confusing or misleading memo can mess up an organization. Don't let it happen on your watch. Memos matter. Take them seriously. The same admonition applies to electronic messages as well.

CYBER STRAIGHT TALK:
MAKING THE MOST OF ELECTRONIC MESSAGES

The average U.S. office worker receives 201 phone, paper, and e-mail messages a day.

—Real Simple

Electronic messaging has revolutionized the way school systems (and other organizations) do business. Thanks to e-mail, voice mail, copiers, and fax machines, teachers, principals, and superintendents now have many new ways and opportunities to say the right thing. Or the wrong thing.

It's not all good news, however. E-mail has become the bureaucrat's best friend and electronic junk mail has become epidemic. Some administrators send unsolicited e-mail messages simply to show others they are still around.

Answering e-mail and other electronic messages can now consume large chunks of a school leader's time. Unfortunately, even a useless message beckons for a response. There may be such a thing as too much electronic messaging. In Iceland, the term *pager* translates as "thief of peace." That's why the country has banned the term. They may be on to something there.

The problem of e-mail overload has become so bad that some U.S. companies now shut down all high-tech communication for an hour a day so that employees have to deal with each other directly, up close and personal. Is there a lesson for schools here?

Even though electronic messages are instant and informal, they shouldn't be treated casually. Some electronic communications have more impact than others, simply because some administrators know how to use the new medium better than others. You want to be in the know-how group.

Informality and immediacy are no excuse for sloppiness. As it turns out, the old rules for written communication apply to e-mail as well. In addition, savvy school leaders understand that a whole new protocol or etiquette ("netiquette") has to be developed for the use of electronic messaging. If you want to get the biggest bang for your e-mail buck, certain rules apply:

- Always have a real reason for sending your e-mail messages. Don't become an e-pest by adding to the garbage heap of worthless communications. ("Half of work-related e-mail has no discernible value." —Craig Contoni) Useless mail disrupts and interrupts real work.
- Reserve e-mail for informal messages. It is not a viable medium for heavy, sensitive content.
- Don't hide behind e-mail to avoid face-to-face contact or confrontation.

- Refrain from putting anything in an e-mail message that you would not say in person or want others to read. Never assume confidentiality of electronic messaging.
- Don't send frivolous, extraneous, or unnecessary messages.
- Organize before sending any kind of electronic message. Put good news first and try to end on a positive note.
- Choose your e-mail words carefully. You can't retrieve them once they are sent.
- If you have to e-mail bad news:
  1. Start with a buffer.
  2. Give reasons behind the bad news.
  3. State the bad news clearly.
  4. Close with hope.
- Follow the standard format for e-mail messages:
  1. Limit line length to between sixty and eighty characters.
  2. Limit paragraphs to a maximum of eight lines.
  3. Use spaces instead of indenting.
  4. Use a standard font. (Fancy fonts can distract from the message.)
- Visualize the person(s) you are sending the message to. It helps you communicate easily and comfortably.
- Write naturally and concisely. Avoid run-on messages.
- Keep sentences short (fifteen to twenty words at most).
- Seek clarity by sticking to familiar words and shunning unknown technical terms.
- Always use the subject line to signal the message's content.
- Include a greeting (appropriate salutation) and closing.
- Be courteous. "Please" and "thank you" are always e-appropriate.
- Indicate what type of response is anticipated or desired.

- Bring closure to your message. Don't leave the reader wondering if there is more to come.
- Limit the use of uppercase letters. It's like shouting in someone's ear.
- Don't let the informality of e-mail lure you into being overly familiar or chummy.
- Never use profanity or obscenities in an e-mail message.
- Don't use e-mail to spread gossip or rumors.
- Remember that e-mail is not an appropriate vehicle for personal or classified ads.
- Conduct your love life in person on your own time, not on the school's e-mail.
- Try not to leave messages late on Friday. Most people don't like having a big backlog of e-mail messages first thing on Monday morning.
- Always double-check spelling and grammar before sending an e-mail message.
- Avoid "flame mail" (e-mail written in anger).
- Use emoticons—:) for a smile or :(for a frown—sparingly.
- Limit the number of attached documents.
- Make it a point to reply to all e-mail messages within twenty-four hours.

Effective school leaders use e-mail as a tool, not a toy. Writing is writing whether it's handwritten or keyboarded. Electronic messaging only multiplies your opportunities to get your messages across.

That's why more and more school leaders are using "blogs" (web logs—personal electronic journals) to create a more informal and intimate way to keep parents, patrons, and the public better informed on inside issues, plans, and actions. Sometimes, blogs can include relevant information that doesn't quite fit any other more traditional communication medium.

To ensure maximum viewership and effectiveness, veteran bloggers offer the following suggestions (do's and don'ts):

Do's

- Remember that informal doesn't mean unprofessional.
- Keep the log up-to-date. Change information frequently.
- Keep it simple. Too much clutter is distracting.
- Write about what's interesting, informative, and useful to viewers, not just what you care about.
- Keep in mind that ANYONE (any age) can access your blog and a blog message is forever.

Don'ts

- Include anything that might embarrass or harm you or others.
- Put in anything you wouldn't want your mother to read.
- Use too many technical terms.
- Try to be too cute, chummy, or "cool."
- Include anyone's name without permission.

As in all writing, how you say the right thing is as important as saying it in the first place. It's as true for easy-access e-mail as it is for formal report writing.

REAL-WORLD REPORT WRITING

The farther you climb up the administrative ladder, the more reports you are responsible for. If you're lucky, you may get someone else to write some of them for you. Usually, you have to do them yourself. Get used to it.

Many administrators don't like to prepare reports. They are not always fun to write. They are not always fun to read. But, often, they are the only way to get the staff, the district administration, the school board, or the community to pay attention.

Good reports don't have to be poetic, slick, glossy, thick, or pretty. They just have to be clear. The best reports are Spartan. The leaner they are, the more likely they are to be read, understood, accepted, and acted upon.

The right thing to say in any formal report is precisely what the title of the document calls for. Nothing more. Nothing less. The right way to say it is cleanly and clearly.

Good reports are to the point. They deal with facts, data, analyses, findings, results, conclusions, summaries, and recommendations. That's it. Anything else is needless filler.

The good news is that any school leader, including you, can learn to be an effective report-writer. Actually, you have no choice. Reports are a necessary tool of the craft.

The trick is to tackle each report as you do any other task, by breaking it down into manageable bits and pieces. Most successful reports include a combination of the elements in Box 7.2.

Box 7.2   Elements of an Effective Technical Report*

Cover letter

Foreword

Preface

Acknowledgments

Table of contents

Executive summary (abstract)

Introduction

Data

Analyses

Results/Findings

Conclusions

Recommendations

Summary

Appendices

Bibliography

*No single report has to contain all of these components. Every effective report, however, includes most of them.

Plan each report-writing project carefully and then merely work your way through the plan step-by-step, following these basic principles:

- Be sure the report is necessary. Write for a real-world reason, not just because it's always been done or to fill someone's file.
- For the best results, ask yourself these questions:
  1. Is the information really needed?
  2. Who needs it?
  3. Why?
  4. How will the report be used?
  5. Is there any better way to convey the information?
- Start gathering data as soon as possible.
- Narrow and refine your topic. Stay focused. The hallmark of a successful report is to have a clearly stated purpose and to stick to it. Take time refining the title. It will drive the rest of the report.
- Develop a key sentence. Build on it throughout the report.
- Follow a logical and sequential format.
- Write for your readers. Keep a picture of your intended audience in mind as you write. Write at their level of sophistication. Give them only the information they need.
- Don't show off. A technical report isn't the place for flowery prose or showcasing your vocabulary of obscure words. Plain language and short sentences work best. (Where have you heard that before?)
- Always give full credit to all who contribute to the report.
- Include sufficient details, but avoid overkill.
- Take a lesson from journalists. Organize your material tightly. Put the most important information first and provide supporting detail later on or in the appendices.
- Remember, volume can be your enemy. People—even school board members—won't read lengthy reports.

- Choose words carefully. Take your time. Pick "the right word, not its second cousin" (—Mark Twain). Search for the right word, not just the "somewhat correct" one.
- Avoid use of acronyms or abbreviations. Screen for sexist language.
- Minimize clichés. Avoid slang.
- Trade off adjectives and adverbs for more action words.
- Simplify all data, statistics, and graphics as much as possible without sacrificing accuracy.
- Make your recommendations razor-sharp—impossible to be misunderstood.
- Proofread carefully. Try reading the manuscript out loud.
- Complete reports in a timely manner. If you miss the window of opportunity, you've wasted your time and effort.

Once the basic writing is completed, consider adding touches that can significantly enhance the impact of any written report.

Besides content, appearance has a lot to do with how a report is received. If it looks good at first glance, people are more likely to read it thoroughly. Experienced technical writers always look for ways to improve the eye appeal and readability of their work by

- Choosing an appealing format (e.g., two columns, three columns).
- Using wide margins and leaving ample space at the top and bottom of each page. White space isn't wasted space. It helps break up the printed page and adds to the visual appeal of the overall report. Crowded pages turn readers off.
- Including uncluttered graphics.
- Making liberal use of highlights, bold headings, boxes, and bullets where appropriate to increase interest and emphasis.

As you can tell from these tips, report writing isn't exactly an art form. It's just straight talk—with backup. You may not like to do it. Do it anyway.

Only fools pass up a good opportunity to get the right message through to the right parties at the right time. That's what effective technical reports can do for you.

How to Say the Right Thing in Business Letters

CEOs and other corporate leaders have always known that business letters can be powerful communication tools. School leaders need to learn the same lesson.

It should be no surprise that writing good business letters isn't as easy as it looks, because a lot has to be covered in a short space. Business letters can be used to inform, instruct, inspire, reason with, convince, coax, coach, or cajole a variety of audiences. That's a lot to expect from a few scraps of paper (preferably a single sheet).

Fortunately, help is available in the form of comprehensive collections of model letters prepared by professional educators (see Resource C).

Unfortunately, the models seldom match the exact circumstances you're dealing with in the real world. Even if you develop your own portfolio of form letters for use in your unique school setting, they can't match every situation. In many cases, you will end up having to write your own business letters basically from scratch.

Consequently, if you want to write better school business letters (who wouldn't?), here's how to do it:

- Pay attention to other administrators' letters. Notice what works and what doesn't. There's no law against borrowing ideas. It's called learning.
- Think before you write. It never hurts.
- Include all the standard components of an effective business letter (see Boxes 7.3 and 7.4).

Box 7.3   Anatomy of an Effective Business Letter

1. Connect: Establish who you are.
2. State the purpose of the letter.
3. Explain relevant background information.
4. Make clear what you want. (Don't leave readers wondering, "So what?")

Box 7.4   Sample School Business Letter

Dear_____:

As principal of the high school, I appreciated your honesty in sharing your views about student athletic fees last night. Open communication is the key to a healthy home-school partnership.

I agree that these fees are too high. Since the fees are set annually by the school board, I will continue to lobby board members to lower these charges. I hope you will do the same. If enough parents, patrons, and staff members complain, I am confident a solution can be found.

In the meantime, I want to remind you that we have scholarships available to cover the fees for students who can't afford them. As long as I am principal, no student will be prevented from participating for financial reasons.

If you know of any student who needs such help, please let me know. You can be assured we will waive their fees and handle the matter with discretion and strict confidentiality.

Thanks again for voicing your concern. Please feel free to contact me in the future if you have other questions or suggestions. We rely on involved parents like you to help us better meet the needs of all students in our school.

Sincerely,

_____

- Except for legal correspondence, adopt an informal style. Write as you speak.
- Keep the tone of your letters professional and friendly. Strive to be helpful.
- Be direct. Refuse to say anything in a roundabout way.
- Take the reader's feelings into account.
- Don't overuse the word I. Emphasize you and we instead.
- Strive for a strong beginning. You often hook or lose the reader within the first sentence or two.
- Introduce yourself right away.
- Avoid stuffy language.
- Omit all extraneous or irrelevant words, ideas, or material. Be tough about this.
- Remain nonjudgmental.
- Don't attempt to threaten or intimidate the reader.
- If you have a choice, opt for monosyllabic words.
- Don't oversell your point. There's truth in the old joke: If someone asks what time it is, don't go into how a clock works.
- End on a positive or encouraging note if possible.
- Use a postscript (P.S.) for any point you want to emphasize or highlight. Many people read the P.S. position of a letter first.
- Take time to edit and make corrections. The goal is to make your correspondence "letter perfect." Don't be afraid to use a dictionary if needed.
- A good business letter is only as long as it needs to be. If at all possible, limit your business letters to one page.

Business letters aren't just correspondences you have to write. They should be letters you want to write as leader of the school community.

Of course, the most welcome letter is always the one a person never expected to receive. That's why the school leaders you admire most make it a habit to surprise people with letters of praise, appreciation, or gratitude (these are always the right things to say in any situation). It's another way to gain an edge.

CORRECT FORMS OF ADDRESS FOR LETTERS TO SPECIAL PUBLIC FIGURES

Before you can say the right thing or get your point across in any school business letter, you have to get the recipient's attention. When communicating verbally, you do this with a greeting. In writing, you have to do it with a proper salutation. That's why it pays to know the correct form of address to use in every letter—particularly when dealing with special public figures.

School leaders who have to correspond with all kinds of people—including legislators, members of Congress, governors, judges, and church officials—can start off on the right foot simply by addressing the parties properly.

Using the right form of address won't guarantee the reader's attention and acceptance, but using the wrong form is likely to ensure that the reader will be turned off from the very beginning. Why take chances?

Proper protocol calls for using the following forms of address in formal correspondence to selected officials:

- Political Officials

    Senator (U.S. or state)
    Addressing the letter: The Hon. Jane Smith
    Salutation: Dear Senator Smith
    or   Dear Senator

    Representative (U.S. or state)
    Addressing the letter: The Hon. Joe Smith
    Salutation: Dear Mr. Smith
    or   Dear Rep. Smith

or	Dear Congressman (U.S. only)

Governor
| Addressing the letter | The Hon. Joe Smith |
| Salutation: | Dear Governor Smith |

Judge
Addressing the letter:	The Hon. Joe Smith
Salutation:	Dear Sir
or	Dear Judge Smith

- Members of the Clergy

  Priest or Minister
  | Addressing the letter: | The Rev. Joe Smith |
  | Salutation: | Dear Rev. Smith |

  Rabbi
  | Addressing the letter: | Rabbi Jane Smith |
  | Salutation: | Dear Rabbi Smith |

- Military Personnel

  Commissioned Officer
  | Addressing the letter: | Col. Joe Smith |
  | Salutation: | Dear Col. Smith |

Using the right form of address in correspondence with public figures isn't being fussy. It's a sign of respect. You can never go wrong being respectful.

HOW TO WRITE STRAIGHT-TO-THE-POINT PRESS RELEASES AND NEWS ITEMS

The media have a nose for bad news in the school. You have to help them sniff out the good news. Some school leaders have good luck using press releases to get their message out to the community.

Press releases allow you to try to get out what you want others to know, as opposed to reporter interviews that merely get out what others think they ought to know.

Of course, the right thing to say in press releases is something newsworthy. To determine if what you have to say qualifies as "news," ask if it meets these criteria:

- Is it something out of the ordinary?
- Are there unusual aspects to the story?
- Is the story of interest to anyone besides parents?
- Do you have all the relevant facts?
- Would a significant number of the general public identify with the story?
- Are there any photo ops (opportunities) associated with the story?

If your information passes these tests, a press release can be an effective way to disseminate it to a large audience. If it doesn't meet the newsworthiness standard, look for another means of getting the word out.

What appeals to many school leaders is that you don't have to be a journalism major to write successful press releases. They are relatively easy to prepare. There are just a few necessary rules to guide you in preparing a statement for the press or other media. Here they are:

- Be sure your press releases are well written, tightly focused, and easy to read (see Box 7.5).
- Anticipate questions and try to cover all the bases.
- Put all the important stuff early in the article—preferably in the first paragraph.
- Make a point to include all the essential information:
  1. Who
  2. What
  3. Where
  4. When
  5. Why
  6. How
  7. Whom to contact for more details

- Include actual names and quotations whenever possible. It adds human-interest appeal.
- Double-check all names, dates, and spellings for accuracy.

Box 7.5   Sample Press Release

NEWS RELEASE For Immediate Release
Contact Person: Frank Lead, Principal
Phone Number: (444) 777-1234

BOMB THREAT PRANK AVERTED

Thanks to quick action by school personnel, a bomb threat evacuation of CORWIN HIGH SCHOOL was handled as a routine fire drill on Friday afternoon. Most students were unaware of anything out of the ordinary.

At 2 p.m. on Friday, the school office received an anonymous bomb threat. Following the school's predetermined emergency plan, students were quickly evacuated to a site a safe distance from the school while the police bomb squad searched the building and grounds for any suspicious devices. None were found.

Police officials credit the school's quick response time with avoiding any undue panic among students or staff members. This is the third bomb threat received by the school in the past two years. No actual bombs have been found to date, but each threat is taken seriously and handled according to district guidelines for emergency action.

"Most bomb threats are hoaxes, but they aren't a joke," explains Police Chief John Star. "Anyone with information about this latest incident should contact city police immediately," the chief added.

Principal Frank Lead commented that today's unscheduled fire drill actually served as a wake-up call and a good introduction for next week's Fire Safety Program, which will involve all students in learning the latest fire prevention and emergency safety measures.

(Note: This sample release is quoted from *Lead, Follow, or Get Out of the Way*, Ramsey, 2006.)

Of course, even if you do everything by the numbers, there is no guarantee that the media will print or broadcast your story. If not, have a backup plan for disseminating the information and try again later with another story.

Be patient. When the media have space to fill and are looking for a good story, be ready to fill the gap with more good news about what's happening in your school.

Every favorable story or article you get printed or aired reaches large numbers of people at no cost to the school. It's better and cheaper than a paid ad. You can't beat that price. It's worth putting up with a little frustration and a few rejections.

Finally, the real message of this chapter is simply that, whether you are writing letters, reports, memos, or manuscripts, plain English and straight talk should be your constant companion. In school or in life, you can't find any better communication tools to help you say the right thing in all situations.

How to Say the Right Thing With Gestures and Body Language

The body is the communication channel over which we have the least control and understand the least, but has the most impact.

—Sue Morem

I n his book, *How to Make People Like You in 90 Seconds or Less,* Nicholas Boothman suggests that you can get anyone to like you and listen to you almost immediately, simply by adopting their body language and voice tone. When you synchronize your body movements to another's (e.g., lean when they lean and sway when they sway), without mimicking them, Boothman says you put them at ease so they will be more receptive to you and what you have to say.

According to Boothman, adjusting your body language to be in sync with others is almost a surefire way to make a favorable first impression within seconds. Wow! If this is true, there's a lesson here for school leaders.

When bodies talk, people listen—and believe what they hear (see). You need to know this the next time and every time you try to get your point across to a new individual or audience. As it turns out, the body has a language of its own. It pays to learn its vocabulary.

How the "Silent Language" Speaks Volumes

Sometimes, even if you listen to everything that is said, you may still miss half the conversation. We don't communicate with just words. We also speak with gestures. We use hands and bodies and the way we stand, posture, or move to help us say the right thing.

Body language and nonverbal messages make up a "silent language" that communicates just as much as—maybe more than—our spoken words.

Some experts calculate that as much as 60% of all communication is nonverbal. They also estimate that human beings are capable of exhibiting

- 700,000 different physical signs
- 5,000 different hand gestures
- 1,000 different postures

That's a lot of body talk. There may be a reason why babies learn to smile and make gestures before they learn any spoken words.

It's no surprise, then, that many of the strongest and clearest messages are not carried by spoken or written words, but by silent cues and clues. Nonverbal messages (i.e., gestures, posture, facial expressions, nervous movements, etc.) really do speak louder than words.

Some of the most common, familiar, and revealing body signals include:

- A wrinkled forehead
- Raised eyebrows
- Rapid blinking
- Evasive eye movements
- A tightly drawn mouth
- Facial tics
- Straining neck muscles
- Slouched shoulders
- Finger tapping
- Crossed arms
- Foot tapping
- Irregular breathing
- Perspiring

Such nonverbal communicators are *powerful* because people automatically pick up on them and just naturally know what they mean. Body signals are intrinsically credible and believable.

Almost every part of your body is capable of sending signals that may belie the words you speak. Words can deceive, but the body seldom lies. Most of us can control what we say, but not our body talk. Who can regulate their blinking, breathing, and perspiring?

Gestures or other body signals can be intuitive or learned behaviors. In either case, they usually occur simultaneously—often unconsciously and involuntarily. That's why it is virtually impossible to mask the messages the body sends out.

Effective school leaders make sure they are not betrayed by body language. Instead, they intentionally use gestures and other body signals to help them make their point and say what they mean. The best school leaders know (where many also-rans and wannabes don't) that straight talk requires no-nonsense nonverbal communication as much as plain verbal language

The secret is to make sure that your words, your tone, and your body language all say the same thing.

AVOID SENDING MIXED MESSAGES

Just like everyone else, educators are frequently unaware of the multitude of messages their bodies are constantly conveying, but other people are not. That's why all of us are sometimes guilty of sending out mixed messages through unintended inconsistencies and contradictions between our words and our nonverbal signals (see Box 8.1).

When your words don't match your body language, students, parents, and others quickly become confused and distrustful. When confronted with two sets of signals, most people tend to believe the one they see, rather than what they hear.

Box 8.1 Examples of Inconsistent Verbal and Nonverbal Communication

Verbal Message	Contradictory Nonverbal Signal
I'm open to suggestions.	Folded arms
I take your ideas seriously.	Rolling eyes
This is terrible.	Hint of a grin
I'll help all I can.	Backing away
I'm not surprised.	Arched eyebrows

That's why, whenever it is important to send a clear, unmistakable message (when isn't it important?), it is crucial that your verbal and nonverbal signals remain in sync by following two simple rules:

1. Be sure your nonverbal signals are sending the message you intend. (Is your body saying what you want it to say?)

2. Be sure your nonverbal signals are consistent with your verbal message. (Are your body and your tongue saying the same thing?)

It's easy to be oblivious to the silent signals your body sends out. That's why it is easy to be misunderstood or misinterpreted and why it is difficult to deceive an audience. Body language is a phony's worst enemy. Other people read your body language loud and clear, whether you do or not.

Effective school leaders have to tune in to nonverbal messages (both their own and other people's) to avoid giving off confusing signals. Believability and credibility depend on seeing to it that your words and your body language say the same thing and say what you mean every time.

The principle of straight talk applies to the silent language of nonverbal communication as well as to spoken or written expression. The school leaders who communicate best with all their diverse publics know this and act on it every day. Do you? It starts by learning the language of the body.

UNDERSTANDING THE VOCABULARY OF BODY LANGUAGE

The science of kinetics (body language) tells us that the body never shuts up. Even when you bite your tongue to keep from speaking, your body keeps right on talking. Sometimes, it tells more than you want people to know.

From head to toe, your body is constantly emitting some kind of message (e.g., tension, fatigue, boredom, attraction, or calmness).

Although all body parts are used to send out nonverbal messages (see Box 8.2), the face, mouth, and eyes are the most expressive communicators.

Most experts agree that there are six (seven, if you count embarrassment) basic facial expressions (fear, anger, sadness, disgust, surprise, and happiness), but some postulate that people can exhibit a range of up to 7,000 different facial signals.

Box 8.2   Nonverbal Message Centers

Nonverbal clues and cues emanate from all these sources:	
Hands	Nostrils
Eyes	Forehead
Eyebrows	Shoulders
Lips	Spine
Jaw	Mouth
Arms	Muscles

As with other body parts and movements, some facial messages are positive (smile, laughter, wink) and some are negative (frown, sneer, glare). Obviously, managing nonverbal messages starts by controlling facial communication.

Body positions and movements (including facial expressions) can work for or against the message you intend to send. Some help focus attention on what you are trying to say (see Box 8.3). Some are merely distractions (see Box 8.4). Focused is better.

Box 8.3   Focused Body Movements

Positive
Open arms
Relaxed stance
Moving closer
Leaning forward
Touching

Negative
Pointing
Jabbing
Throwing up hands
Fist pounding
Rude gestures

Box 8.4   Distracting Body Movements

- Constant fidgeting
- Shifting weight from foot to foot
- Scratching
- Finger tapping
- Face stroking
- Shoulder shrugging
- Knuckle cracking

One of the keys to effective communication is understanding what different body movements mean. Once you learn the vocabulary of body language, you can "read" what other people are really saying and use your own silent language to enhance and reinforce your verbal messages. Part of saying the right thing is showing the public appropriate nonverbal signals that coincide with what your mouth is saying.

Decoding nonverbal messages is mostly a matter of paying attention. Once you are aware of the basics, you can learn to recognize the meaning of most body movements. For starters, following is a brief introductory course in nonverbal communication (Body Language 101):

- Showing the palms of your hands signals that you have nothing to hide.
- Flaring nostrils represent anger.
- A quivering chin usually means sorrow.
- Direct eye contact conveys interest, sincerity, truthfulness, and honesty. Nobody believes shifty eyes. (One trick used by some school leaders is to make it a point to note the eye color of each person they want to communicate with.)
- A big smile and a hearty handshake depict joy—even jubilation.

- Frowns, downcast eyes, and/or drooping shoulders mean depression or displeasure.
- Sweaty palms are a sign of fear, nervousness, or untruthfulness. (Lie detectors count on this involuntary reaction.)
- Clenched teeth can mean fear, pain, or determination.
- Exposing the heart by unbuttoning or opening a jacket or vest or touching the heart indicates openness.
- Adjusting clothing suggests discomfort and nervousness.
- Tension is often manifested by a stiffened posture or throbbing neck veins.
- Touching or stroking the hair can be a sign of attraction or flirtation.
- Sucking in the stomach indicates an attempt to appear younger or more attractive.
- Folded hands denote peacefulness.
- Yawning—well, we all know what a yawn means.
- Touching the nose or rubbing the eyes is often interpreted as a sign of lying or having something to hide.
- Excessive blinking indicates fear of discovery.
- A lowered head or eyes suggest unapproachability.
- Crossing legs at the ankle sends a message of insecurity.
- Crossing arms or putting hands on hips suggests resistance or defiance.
- Leaning forward indicates interest. Conversely, leaning backward or moving away signals lack of interest or withdrawal.

Obviously, the examples above are illustrative and suggestive rather than exhaustive. But they give you the idea. You can take it from there.

Deciphering the vocabulary of body language requires an alertness to visible signs, awareness of what's going on at the moment, and some commonsense interpretation. These are all things good school leaders are known for.

Once you can recognize the body messages other people are sending out, you can more readily take charge of your own. A good way to begin is by controlling your everyday gestures and putting them to work for you to help say the right thing every time.

USING THE POWER OF GESTURES

Gestures are powerful. They can enhance, animate, underscore, reinforce, punctuate, and/or energize your verbal messages. They provide shortcut signals to your true meaning. Gestures work because they are familiar to most people and immediately recognizable (see Box 8.5).

Box 8.5   Common Gestures in the United States

High fives
Thumbs up (or down)
OK sign
V for victory
T for time-out
Hang-loose sign
Throw up hands (in disgust)
Raise hands and arms (I surrender)
"The finger" (the f-word of gesturing)
Thumbing the nose
Beckoning finger
Waving
Winking
Outstretched open hand, held vertically (stop)
Finger to lips (shhh)
Blessing gesture (common among Catholics and other
     religious groups)
Finger drawn across throat (cut or stop)
Pointing to head and rotating finger (you're crazy)

The trick is to match your gestures to your message. The larger your audience, the more expansive and sweeping your gestures should be. Up close, facial gestures (sticking out tongue, rolling eyes, etc.) work well; at a distance, hand gestures are more effective.

It is always wise to pay attention to what your hands are doing. Next to the face, the hands are viewed as the most revealing nonverbal signal-senders. If your hand gestures contradict your spoken words, you've lost your audience (whether it's one person or a whole roomful).

The best overall advice is to use open gestures as much as possible in order to engage your listeners, win approval for what you are saying, and get the audience on your side.

Obviously, gestures are great tools for helping to get your message and meaning across, but they also can get you into deep trouble. All people use gestures. Unfortunately, however, the same gestures don't always mean the same thing in different cultures or to different groups.

STAY OUT OF TROUBLE: AVOID THE PITFALLS OF DIFFERENT MEANINGS FOR DIFFERENT GROUPS

Gestures aren't universal in their meaning. Sometimes, they even have contradictory meanings in different cultures. That's why it's easy to get into trouble simply by using inappropriate gestures. When this happens, claiming innocence, ignorance, or good intentions won't help. This is especially true of public figures, such as school leaders, who have to deal with diverse ethnic and cultural groups every day.

Using the right gesture with the wrong group is a surefire way to be misunderstood, disbelieved, or rejected outright. Meaningful gestures boost understanding. Misconstrued gestures only anger and alienate an audience.

We've all heard stories of Native American children who have been misunderstood or mishandled by school officials just because they resist making direct eye contact, which is a sign of disrespect in their culture.

This is just one example of varied interpretation or application of a body signal. There are many more. Here are some you may not know about:

- Nodding the head up and down means "no" in Bulgaria.
- The thumbs-up gesture is considered vulgar in Iran and Australia. In Japan, it signifies the number "5," not necessarily approval.
- Greeks sometimes smile when they are angry.
- A firm handshake is interpreted as a sign of aggression in some countries.
- The OK gesture is considered rude in Germany.
- Standing with your hands in your pockets is bad manners in Belgium.
- The Dutch pat the back of one hand with the fingers of the other to indicate that someone is gay.
- In Turkey, showing the sole of your shoe is an insult.
- It is unladylike for women to cross their legs in Spain
- Pointing to the eyes means "You can't fool me" in parts of France.
- Patting a child on the head is sacrilegious in India.
- Pounding a fist into a cupped hand is a vulgar gesture in Brazil.

The list could go on and on. "Different strokes for different folks" is more than a cliché when it comes to gestures. It's a fact of life.

School officials who want to avoid communication catastrophes care enough to learn the cultural differences in gestures among minority groups with whom they interact on a regular basis. If you head up a diverse school or district, you can't afford not to. It's too easy to get into trouble by accident, without bringing it on yourself.

The answer is to always be aware, observant, and sensitive. And ask or check out what common gestures mean to different groups before ever meeting with or addressing them.

Making the effort to learn the language of gestures used by groups you frequently associate with is a sign of respect. It's common courtesy. It's good business. It's good leadership. And it's another way to ensure that you say the right thing.

SMILE, YOU REALLY ARE ON CANDID CAMERA

There is one universal gesture that cuts across all barriers. It works every time, everywhere. It's a smile.

Nothing works better to warm up an audience, engage a single listener, establish rapport, or pave the way for effective communication than a smile.

As a teacher, principal, or superintendent, you are always in the public eye whether you are aware of it or not. When people see you smiling, they have positive feelings about you that often carry over to the school. That's why a smile is a perfect public relations gesture. It's free. It's equally accessible to everyone. And you can count on it.

Take a tip from some of the most successful school leaders: Use your smile—a lot! Work on it. Perfect it. When in doubt, let it out. You can't go wrong smiling. A pleasant smile is always the right thing to say.

The bottom line is that using the right gesture and properly managing your body's signals can spell the difference between making your point and missing the mark.

If you still doubt that body language is important, just ask for a show of hands—oops. Even that is a form of body talk.

Body language is everywhere. It's all around you all the time. It's too good a tool to ignore. You are less of a leader than you should be if you don't use the body's silent signals to your advantage.

Dare to let your body speak for you. It knows what you want to say and sometimes can say it better than spoken words ever can.

How to Target Communication to All Stakeholders

Precision in communication is important, more important than ever, in an era of hair-trigger balances, where a false or misunderstood word may create as much disaster as a sudden thoughtless act.

— James Thurber

Throughout the preceding chapters, this guide has stressed that communication is the life's blood of every successful school. Like all public institutions, schools should be transparent. Information belongs to everyone.

Vital data and other information should not be hidden or hoarded by a select few or rationed out as a reward or perk for favored individuals or groups. Everyone deserves to be kept in the loop. That's why, in the most productive schools, communication isn't spotty or sporadic; it is a constant, even flow.

If the school—your school—is going to work for everyone and everyone work for the school, all parties are entitled to play with the same full deck of information, rather than being dealt separate and different hands.

As leader of the school, it's your role to communicate appropriately with all stakeholders, not just the students and staff inside the organization. Or not just the parents outside of the school. But everyone—including senior citizens, families with no children, politicians, business leaders, new residents, refugees, immigrants, boosters, critics, friends, foes, reformers—everyone. The problem is that there is no one right way to say the right thing to all stakeholders.

TALE OF THE TAIL: CUSTOMIZING COMMUNICATION

The tricky challenge is that each group of stakeholders has unique and distinctive communication needs. In communicating effectively with all the various components of the school, no one size fits all anymore. Today, school leaders have to differentiate their communication approaches and target each group individually.

Some humorists claim the thermos bottle is one of the greatest inventions in history, because it keeps hot things hot and cold things cold—and knows "when to which." Like it or not, school administrators today must learn the lesson of the thermos bottle. Not only do they need to know and use all the broad array of communication strategies and techniques pinpointed throughout this guide, they also need to know when to use which approach with each individual constituency.

Fortunately, customizing communication may not be as difficult as you might imagine. After all, hunting dogs do it all the time. Did you know that a trained retriever's tail points one way for grouse and another way for pheasants and straight down for game buried in overgrowth?

I don't know if you can teach an old dog new tricks or not; but, hopefully, educators can learn a trick or two about communication from our retriever friends. If a dog can differentiate communication based on the target audience, surely school leaders can do it as well.

Professional educators have finally learned how to differentiate instruction to accommodate individual differences. Now, it's time to learn how to differentiate communication to reach varied audiences.

We all know the old definition: "Insanity is repeating the same action and expecting different results." The corollary for communication is: "Insanity is repeating the same communication approach with different groups and expecting the same results with all groups." One uniform communication strategy doesn't work anymore (if it ever did). It's long past time for school leaders to tailor communication to different target publics.

OLD STAND-BYS AREN'T GOOD ENOUGH

Principals and superintendents can no longer count on traditional communication stand-bys. It is not enough merely to rely on articles in the local newspaper and a periodic school newsletter sent to all households to get the school's message across.

It is not the same world that many school administrators grew up in, where everyone read the daily newspaper and paid attention to mailings from the school. Today, many parents and other community members don't subscribe to a newspaper, let alone actually read it. They rely, instead, on the Internet, satellite radio, or cable television to get the news.

To complicate matters further, in a growing number of homes in every city and town, the adults can't read English. In these cases, a school newsletter is more a source of confusion and consternation than of communication and information.

There is simply no one method, manner, mode, or medium of communication that works to say the right thing to everyone every time. It is no longer a matter of choosing a preferred approach to communicating; it is about using every approach imaginable (and a few you can't imagine) to find what works best for each audience.

NEW TOOLS FOR SAYING THE RIGHT THING TO EVERYONE

The need to channel communication in varied ways to an increasingly diverse clientele has led many school leaders to explore some unorthodox, unusual, and previously untapped tools.

Not only are administrators making greater use of modern everyday technology (e.g., cell phones, text messaging, e-mail, cable TV, and fax machines); but most now have their own school Web site.

Obviously, Web sites are the wave of the future. A school without a Web site is like a special event with no advance advertising—no one knows much about it and few plan to show up.

Of course, not all Web sites are useful. A "blah," ho-hum Web site is worse than no Web site. Most experienced web-masters agree that effective school Web sites feature easy navigation (easy to find and follow) and worthwhile content (information that is interesting, accurate, up-to-date, and devoid of "educationese").

In addition to creating engaging Web sites, some school leaders are taking use of the Internet to the next level by adding another dimension of personal communication— "blogging." (See Chapter 7.)

A growing number of public officials, including principals, superintendents, city managers, and even congressmen, have had success using a Web log as an informative diary of daily interest, ideas, and activities, open to the public. Try it. You will be amazed by the number of "hits" an administrator's Web log will attract.

Besides increased Internet use, another creative approach to communication with hard-to-reach audiences is to borrow a page from small businesses by engaging in "guerilla marketing." Many independent business entrepreneurs are now eschewing expensive conventional mass sales techniques and becoming more nimble and flexible by contacting niche markets personally and directly. It can work for school leaders as well.

That's why savvy school officials around the country are picking up on the idea to help reach specific subgroups (e.g., alumni, retirees, drop-outs, immigrant populations, special education parents, families with gifted students, special interest groups, etc.). In schools, guerilla marketing usually involves narrowly focused, hands-on approaches such as

- Writing personal letters (in the appropriate language).
- Distributing targeted brochures in person.
- Taking out yellow page ads.
- Using local access cable TV announcements.
- Purchasing low-budget TV messages in non-prime time.

Another effective (but time-consuming) guerilla marketing strategy is simply to carry the message directly to wherever the target audience tends to congregate, such as hair salons, barbershops, senior centers, coffeehouses, Little League games, class reunions, ethnic festivals, VA hospitals, Special Olympics, or naturalization classes. It's always easier to say the right thing to everyone on their home turf.

The point is that the school is only as strong as its linkages (communication) with all participating groups. Some are difficult to reach. Some don't want to be reached. You have to reach them anyway.

Today's most effective school leaders find a way to send and receive information and conduct a dialogue with all parties. Don't be too proud to employ any conceivable or unconventional communication technique. "Whatever works" is the only standard.

Whenever you are at a loss as to how to reach some group(s), there is one foolproof way to identify what will work. Ask them!

Then, give them the information they want and need in the way they want to get it. Even though it may take extra effort, adaptation, repetition, translation, or interpretation. Differentiating communication always means more work, but it is also always worth it. No one ever said saying the right thing every time was easy.

ONE STRATEGY THAT WORKS WITH ALL STAKEHOLDERS

Fortunately, help is available. There is one secret weapon that makes communication with all types of groups much simpler and easier. It doesn't require any differentiation. It works with all publics and all ages, at all levels, in all situations. It can work in any school. It can work in yours. It works with everyone, every time. It's a wonder that more educators don't use it more often. It's called STRAIGHT TALK! (Remember this from Chapter 1?)

Lack of candor and clarity cost school leaders an enormous amount of credibility and can damage the school's reputation permanently. Yet, educators are notorious for being vague, beating around the bush, hedging on issues, answering in riddles, and speaking in tongues.

It's not a productive approach, because what people—all people—want is simply the plain truth spoken plainly. ("What people really want to hear is the truth." —Winston Churchill) Prize-winning author and former New York City classroom teacher, Frank McCourt, may say it best: "You have to tell the truth or you'll be found out."

Nevertheless, not all administrators tell all the truth all the time or tell it in a way that ordinary folk can readily understand it. Some ignore the truth, stretch the truth, bend the truth, "spin" the truth, or fall back on half-truths.

Worse yet, a few even flat-out lie. We've all known some principals and superintendents who occasionally misrepresent facts to staff, parents, the public—and even the school board and the media. I'm not lying.

It's dangerous, disturbing, stupid, and doesn't work. Messing with the truth is always a monumental mistake. A falsehood is never the right thing to say to any stakeholder. It is always wise to differentiate your communication delivery system, but it is never smart or cool to differentiate the truth.

In addition to total honesty and crystal clarity, straight talk requires using simple and compelling language, sending the same message to all publics and consistently responding to questions in a concise and understandable manner.

How hard is it, then, to speak the truth, speak plainly, and be consistent? Apparently, much more difficult than it sounds, or else straight talk would enjoy much more popular usage among educators, politicians, and bureaucrats.

But despite any difficulty, the most successful school leaders remain huge fans of straight talk because it is the only communication strategy that works with all stakeholders all the time. Straight talk works because

- It builds trust and confidence (while lack of candor and clarity undermines credibility, blocks ideas, impedes action, prevents problem solving, and turns people off).
- It makes everyone an insider.
- It makes conflict resolution and sound decision-making possible.
- It clears the air.
- It allows mistakes and makes saying "I don't know," OK.
- It provides freedom from trying to recall a tangle of falsehoods and fabrications.
- It blasts away denial and promotes reality-based problem solving.
- It leads to action.

- Best of all, it sets the leader and the organization apart. (You can't create a better brand image than truthfulness and straightforward communication.)

With all this going for it, you would think that straight talk would be standard operating procedure for all school officials. It's not. But it can be in your school.

A Seven-Step Code for Saying the Right Thing

If you are truly interested, the easiest and quickest way to make straight talk the language of choice in your school is to adopt the following seven-step communication code:

1. Say only what's true.

2. Say what needs to be said.

3. Say what you mean.

4. Say it to the right people.

5. Say it when it needs to be said (usually the sooner, the better).

6. Say it simply.

7. Say it again. (Keep saying it until everyone "gets it.")

As the head of the school, if you faithfully adhere to this code, people (at all levels) will listen to what you have to say, understand what you have to say, and believe what you say. Better yet, they will buy into the school's message more than ever before. That's good for you, for the school, for the community, and, most important, for the kids.

The challenge, however, is that following a straight-talk communication code isn't easy. If it were, everyone would be doing it. As it turns out, telling the truth, telling it like it is, and telling it so everyone can understand it takes guts.

Plain talk can be embarrassing, uncomfortable, unpopular, unpleasant, and even painful and dangerous. But avoiding the full truth, ducking it, disguising it, distorting it, or covering it up hurts more in the long run and is much more hazardous to the leader and the organization. The fact is that straight talk doesn't create new problems, but it can make new solutions possible.

Nevertheless, many principals and superintendents don't want to face the temporary discomfort, pain, or inconvenience of sticking to the straight-talk code. As pointed out in Chapter 1, a large number of administrators embrace communication tactics and practices that are the antithesis of straight talk, including:

- Hiding behind obfuscation (saying things in the most pompous, puffed-up, and polysyllabic way possible).
- Using euphemisms (stupid substitute terms that don't fool anyone).
- Confusing audiences with technical jargon (educa tors' secret code).
- Burying stakeholders with information overload.
- Sending neutered messages due to excessive political correctness.

Obviously, these approaches are not part of any effective communication code.

If you think I've overstated the case, step back and really listen to your fellow administrators give a speech or participate in a panel discussion at a professional conference, address a student assembly, give a staff pep talk, report to the school board, or answer tough questions from the media. Doesn't much of what they say sound like gobbledygook?

It's not straight talk. It's "bull." Some observers describe listening to educational doublespeak as "Deja Moo"—the feeling that you've heard this bull before.

All of this talk about straight talk underscores the fact that how you communicate can be your best friend or worst enemy. Communication binds the school together. Or not. As a school leader, if you don't get the communication piece right, the rest of the pieces won't fall into place either.

Saying the right thing every time to every constituency is that crucial!

As long as you differentiate the way you deliver information to the school's diverse audiences, stick to straight talk and the seven-step code, and follow the other school-tested communication strategies outlined throughout this guide, you will always have a leg up on the competition.

MORE READY-TO-USE TIPS FOR TARGETING MESSAGES TO SPECIFIC AUDIENCES

If you want more audience-friendly communication tips for targeting messages to diverse groups, shop the list below and take whatever fits your situation:

- Get help. Communication is too important to be left entirely to amateurs (even well-educated amateurs like school principals or superintendents).

  There is a reason why the state of Minnesota doesn't tax advertising. It is considered an essential service for both commercial and consumer interests. It is essential in schools as well.

  If you don't think you need any help with internal and external communication, you don't understand the situation.

  Obviously, different groups prefer to receive information in different ways. They have varying histories, experiences, backgrounds, biases, and frames of reference. Likewise, diverse stakeholders have different levels of understanding of language and sometimes attach different meanings to the same word or phrase (e.g., we all know examples of teenagers using terms in exactly the opposite ways that adults use them).

  Someone needs to understand all this and be able to customize communication accordingly. That's where a communication specialist comes in.

Wherever possible, it pays to bring some professional expertise on board. It can be a full- or part-time position, a consultant, or a qualified volunteer. Whatever works.

Even when hard times hit, don't be too quick to eliminate communication positions. It is during the most troubled periods that you need someone capable of telling the school's story more than ever.

• Pay attention to proofreading all written or printed material coming from the school. This is especially important when sending the same information in different forms to different publics.

The best advice is to refrain from doing the final proofreading of material you've written yourself. An author always tends to "read" what is supposed to be on the page, rather than seeing what actually appears on the page.

One of the quirks of school leadership is that people may not read your message, but they will always spot an error. We all have seen embarrassing examples such as the headline that once appeared in the New Haven, Connecticut, *Register*. It read "Governor's Peni s Busy." It was supposed to read "Governor's Pen Is Busy."

I know how the editor must have felt. Several years ago, I was responsible for releasing an official school publication under the lead, "The _____ Pubic Schools." You don't recover from a gaffe like that overnight.

It may not be fair, but members of all stakeholder groups expect school personnel to be perfect when it comes to spelling, grammar, and punctuation. When we make mistakes, they lose a little confidence in us and we lose a little credibility with them. It's all preventable. It just takes an eye for detail—preferably, someone else's eye.

- Line up translators and interpreters in all the languages represented in your school or district. After all, the first rule of saying the right thing every time is to say it in the right language.

  This signals a welcoming attitude, overcomes language gaps, and builds trust with parents and patrons who do not speak English.

  Fortunately, there are usually numerous sources of potential translators and interpreters in every community, including family, friends, and neighbors of non-English-speaking stakeholders, graduate students majoring in foreign languages, sponsors of immigrant families, and world language teachers from your school and others.

  As a last resort, you may have to rely on the children in the family to translate for their parents, but this can create tensions within the family as traditional roles are reversed.

- Adopt a "no cheap shots" policy. Cheap shots are the bottom feeders of communication. You will always travel farther and faster with all groups if you stick to the high road.

- Try running public service messages in your local movie theatre. Some stakeholders, who seldom read school communications or newspapers, attend movies regularly. A big-screen message is difficult to ignore.

- Avoid overuse of
  1. Axioms (self-evident truths)
  2. Homilies (sermonettes)
  3. Platitudes (banal statements)
  4. Clichés (overused expressions)

  Some groups may not be familiar with the references and will miss the point. More important, all groups grow very tired, very bored, and very annoyed very quickly with these devices.

- Minimize use of acronyms that separate insiders from outsiders. Acronyms are codes that exclude some people. No one should have to decipher messages from the school.
- Choose your vocabulary carefully. Be sure your words fit the audience. In English, some of our words are confusing and don't seem connected to what they mean or represent. In other languages, words more closely convey their true meaning. My favorite example is the Icelandic word for "pager," which is "friopjful" meaning "thief of peace."

   It is also interesting to note that most languages (including English) contain three times as many pessimistic adjectives as the number of optimistic modifiers. This makes it easy to slip into a pattern of pessimistic, negative talk that promotes negative feelings that lead to negative behavior.

   That's why the best school leaders consciously and intentionally avoid falling into the trap of trash talk by emphasizing terms such as "we," "us," "win," and "success" and downplay military metaphors and the vocabulary of violence.

   One sure way to appeal to all levels of stakeholders is to choose and use only positive, understandable words that are consistent with the values of the organization.
- Don't try to be overly cute, clever, funny, or colorful in your language. Some of us remember former news anchor Dan Rather's signature graphic descriptions, such as, "His back's to the wall, his shirttail's on fire, and the bill collector's at the door." But how many of us remember who he was talking about?

   Over-the-top, colorful language is attention-getting, but it can also distract from the intended message. More important, cutesy jokes, folksy metaphors, and idiomatic examples are often lost in translation, causing some audiences to miss the meaning entirely.

- Remember that some groups take longer to "get it" than others. Always repeat and "threepeat" important information, directions, and instructions.
- Run announcements in local foreign language newspapers and on local foreign language radio stations.
- Pay attention to attention span. Some individuals and groups are more focused than others. Not every message can be capsulized in a sound bite, but no message should be so long that you lose your audience either.
- To reach hard-to-reach groups and get them to actively participate in school PTSO, Site Council, or general informational meetings, issue them a specific targeted invitation, schedule meetings at convenient times, serve food, and arrange for free child care. If that fails, try holding meetings on their home turf.
- Your words, formats, and media may vary with different groups, but your attitude toward them should be consistent. Show the same respect for all groups and never talk down to or patronize any cohort of stakeholders.
- Learn all you can about every set of constituents. Overcome your own stereotypes and preconceived biases. You can never communicate effectively with any group as long as you label them or hold generalized misconceptions about who they are and what they want.
- Include leaders of all stakeholder groups (even small minorities) on important school councils, committees, and task forces. They can serve as your eyes, ears, and voice within their specific community.
- Never refuse to meet with any stakeholder group— no matter how radical or controversial they may be. You can't reason or negotiate with people you don't talk to.

- After you've done all you can to communicate with all publics and audiences, know when to shut up!

Whether you pick up on any of the suggestions above or not, you have to pay attention to communication with all constituencies. After all, the quality of your school is tied directly to the quality of your communication with all stakeholders.

HOW TO BE A COMMUNICATIONS HERO

As school leader—more than anyone else—you are the gate keeper, managing the quality, quantity, and flow of information throughout the organization. The point is that the only way to say the right thing every time today is to tailor communication to suit the needs of all the separate groups represented within the school's extended community. (Remember the tale of the tail from man's best friend?)

This doesn't mean telling different tales to different parties. But it does mean giving every group and individual the same straight information and the same straight answers in the way that works best for them.

The trick is to communicate so that it is easy to understand and, therefore, easy to believe what is said. If you do this and nothing else, you will go down in history as a true hero of the organization.

A Final Word

The six steps to becoming a better listener form a ladder:

L: Look at the person speaking to you.

A: Ask questions

D: Don't interrupt.

D. Don't change the subject.

E: Empathize.

R: Respond verbally and nonverbally.

—Georgia Kosmoski and Dennis Pollack (citing Bob Bly)

Preceding chapters have been devoted to helping you and other educators say the right thing and find the right words for all occasions. There is a flip side to this issue that is equally important—it is simply *Not Saying the Wrong Thing*.

Every time you refrain from saying something stupid, gross, tactless, thoughtless, insensitive, hurtful, or dishonest, you enhance your image as a leader.

That's why knowing when to shut up and listen is a survival skill for today's school leaders. If you are like many of us, you should try it more often.

FOR IT IS IN THE LISTENING THAT YOU ARE MOST APT
TO FIND THE RIGHT THING TO SAY EVERY TIME!

Resource A

101 Ways to Be
a Better Communicator
Starting Tomorrow Morning

If you truly want to get better at communicating with the school's diverse publics and audiences, you can do it. And you can start right now. Even if you are already an effective communicator, you can get even better.

But it won't happen just by reading this book. It can happen, however, if you actually apply the advice and strategies in it.

To make it easier to get started, the highlights below have been drawn from the preceding chapters for your quick review. Try them. They work.

Following these commonsense suggestions won't necessarily make you a golden-tongued orator or a Pulitzer Prize-winning writer, but you will see immediate results. No book can promise or deliver more than that.

1. Believe what you say. If you don't, why should anyone else?
2. Make every word count. Fluff and filler can get in the way of your main message.
3. Communicate with confidence and authority. Avoid tentativeness. Certainty works. Waffling doesn't.
4. Take enough time to get your point across. Give others a chance to absorb and assimilate your message.
5. Be willing to speak and write about bad news. It won't get better until you do.

6. Use words that tap into all five senses.
7. Be direct. Cut to the chase.
8. Strive to be natural.
9. Be enthusiastic about what you have to say. Excitement is contagious.
10. Give preference to small, plain words. When communicating, bigger isn't always better.
11. Keep most written sentences short—seventeen words or less usually works best.
12. Know what you are talking or writing about. Otherwise, choose silence.
13. Talk and write more about possibilities and solutions than about problems and excuses.
14. Search for fresh words to convey old news or ideas.
15. Check for understanding frequently.
16. Don't play communication games. Avoid manipulation, hidden agendas, or ulterior motives.
17. Don't whine.
18. Emphasize the words *you* and *we*, and downplay the word *I.*
19. Remember that informality works best in most everyday spoken or written communication.
20. Say what you mean. Don't make people guess at your message or meaning.
21. If one word or sentence will do the job, stop there.
22. Avoid overworked, tired-out words or phrases.
23. Be prepared to repeat important messages—several times.
24. Stay focused. Don't drift while speaking or writing.
25. Prepare. Outline. Rehearse. Visualize what you are going to say. Gather your materials and your thoughts before starting to write.
26. Control your emotions so you can control your words.
27. Avoid labeling students (or adults).
28. Ask for feedback on your communication (spoken or written). "How am I doing?" is always a fair question.
29. Define and clarify all acronyms and abbreviations.
30. Stick to short paragraphs when writing. New paragraphs and intermittent white spaces make your writing more visually appealing and easier to follow and understand.
31. Vary sentence length when writing. It helps keep your readers interested.

32. Don't be afraid to put yourself into your speaking and writing. Be open to self-disclosure. It can help connect you with your audience.

33. Don't make spoken or written promises that you can't keep.

34. Be scrupulously honest—every time! A track record of integrity is the key to credibility and believability.

35. Think about what you are saying. Your mouth should never be on automatic pilot.

36. Always keep your audience members in mind. Look at them if you are speaking. Visualize them if you are writing. Target your message to the specific group involved.

37. Talk with your eyes as well as with your tongue. Make eye contact. If you connect with your eyes, you are more likely to connect with your message.

38. Project. Speak up. Your message won't carry if your voice doesn't.

39. Don't overuse buzzwords.

40. Remove physical barriers when speaking. Get out from behind your desk or podium.

41. Limit the number of messages you try to convey at one time. The most effective communication is a rifle shot, not a shotgun blast.

42. Know when to broadcast and when to tune in. Wait your turn. Don't interrupt others. Only one message can get through at a time.

43. Don't fall into the habit of starting too many sentences with, "There are . . ."

44. Limit the number of qualifiers and modifiers you use.

45. Use metaphors to make your point, but don't mix your metaphors or use ones that are so obscure that no one "gets it."

46. Never speak or write in anger. You will almost always regret it later on.

47. Be alert to nonverbal cues from your audience. They can tell you when to slow down, fast-forward, or shut up.

48. Avoid sweeping generalities. They bounce off, but specificity pierces indifference.

49. Choose the right time to make a point.

50. Practice active listening. Listen for feelings behind the words. They can help you know the right thing to say and how to say it.

51. Never assume that you are being understood or that you understand the other guy.

52. Avoid using too many clichés.

53. Listen to yourself. Edit your own language. Be tough on yourself.
54. Let your passion come through.
55. Don't punctuate every spoken sentence with the phrase, "You know." It's not only immature—it's annoying.
56. Check your tone of voice. Sometimes, it says more than your words.
57. Use vivid language and colorful words to capture the interest of your listeners or readers.
58. Admit it when you are wrong.
59. Apologize promptly when necessary.
60. Be tactful—but direct.
61. Proofread everything you write (including personal notes and letters). Your computer's spell-checker program isn't enough.
62. Don't prejudge other people's intentions or motivations. It can cause you to send the wrong message.
63. Avoid coming across as defensive.
64. Use lots of specific examples. Real-world references work best.
65. Tape-record your speeches and presentations. Use the recordings to identify and eliminate annoying speech mannerisms and habits.
66. Don't overdo scolding students. Find alternatives. Glaring or staring often works as well.
67. Ask for clarification when needed. Urge others to do the same.
68. Don't say or write anything to make fun of or belittle another human being.
69. Avoid overusing the term "whatever." It's not cool. It's adolescent.
70. Adopt a "no cheap shots" policy.
71. Always write from an outline—even if it's only a simple memo. No exceptions.
72. Never use big words just to show off.
73. Keep up-to-date. Don't get caught using yesterday's catch-words or catchphrases.
74. Remember what you have said in the past. It will save you the embarrassment of repeating or contradicting yourself. Even if you don't remember, others will. Remembering is easier if you always tell the truth.
75. Try to write stand-alone memos. Separate subjects deserve separate memorandums.
76. Limit the use of superlatives. Not everything can be *terrific, fabulous,* or *awesome.*

77. Screen out any mixed messages.
78. If you are going to have a dialogue, invite everyone involved.
79. Don't take challenges or opposing views personally.
80. Never tell anyone (student or adult) to "shut up."
81. Don't attempt to write anything when you are hurt, ill, or scared.
82. Remember that attacking another person is not the same thing as presenting a reasonable argument.
83. Don't be afraid to let someone else do your talking or writing for you if they can do it better.
84. Be OK with pauses. Don't feel compelled to fill every period of silence.
85. Use your own words. You can learn from others, but don't steal their words without giving credit.
86. Try to make your audience members glad they listened to or read what you had to say.
87. Keep your sense of humor. Let it show. It can bail you out of a lot of tight situations.
88. Always have a goal (purpose) in mind.
89. Think about the tone of your message. Is it patronizing? Insulting? Does it come across as arrogant? Is it whiney? Is it threatening or intimidating? If so, do something about it.
90. Don't overuse intensifiers such as *very* and *really*.
91. When you are done writing, go back and cut out all extraneous words. They are always there.
92. Be sensitive to cultural differences among individuals and groups.
93. Omit emotional or loaded language that may only heighten disagreement.
94. Avoid argumentative or combative language.
95. Don't demand or require others to listen to or read what you have to say unless there is a good reason.
96. Don't anesthetize your audience. Know when to shut up. Silence can be an effective communication tool too.
97. Know when to stop rewriting or revising. There will always be a better way to say or write something. Do the best you can in the time allowed and move on.
98. Don't put off discussing touchy topics. Procrastination is not a problem-solving technique.
99. Tell everyone the same story.

100. Know when to bite your tongue. For instance, four words always better left unsaid are, "I told you so."
101. Have fun communicating. Lighten up. Don't take yourself or your message too seriously. Education is serious business, but it shouldn't be grim.

Bonus Point: Reread Chapters 1 through 9 as needed.

Resource B

What Others Say About Communication: Quips, Quotes, and Anecdotes

The truth is that there is virtually no case where communications are so good there is no room for improvement.

—Ted Pollack

It is a luxury to be understood.

—Ralph Waldo Emerson

With parents and teachers, you can't go wrong with the shut mouth.

—Frank McCourt

Information voids will be filled by rumors and speculation unless they are preempted by open, credible and trustworthy communication. Pull no punches. When you know an answer, give it. When you don't, say so. When you're guessing, admit it. But don't stop communication.

—Jean B. Keffeler

Stealing someone else's words frequently spares the embarrassment of eating your own.

—Peter Anderson

You will never really know what I mean and I'll never know exactly what you mean.

—Mike Nichols

Syllables govern the world.

—John Selden

To say the right thing at the right time, keep still most of the time.

—John W. Rope

Words, then, are . . . persuaders and fortifiers, tranquilizers and irritants; and they are forces for good or evil—builders and destroyers.

—J. Donald Adams

The medium is the message.

—Marshall McLuhan

Listening, not imitation, may be the sincerest form of flattery.

—Dr. Joyce Brothers

Communication is learned behavior.

—Paul W. Swets

One of the salient features of our culture is that there is so much bullshit.

—Harry G. Frankfurt

Be a good listener. Your ears will never get you into trouble.

—Frank Tyger

Example isn't another way to teach, it is the only way to teach.

—Albert Einstein

What the people really want to hear is the truth—it is an exciting thing—to speak the truth.

—Winston Churchill

More yacking doesn't guarantee understanding.

—Bill Jensen

Has it ever occurred to you how much words have in common with money? They are . . . sometimes inflated and frequently devalued, put in circulation and withdrawn. They, too, accumulate interest, they are coined, they are borrowed, they grow blurred with use, they are hoarded and they are spent lavishly. They can be counterfeit. They convince and they seduce. They are accepted (too often) at face value.

—J. Donald Adams

When communications are effective, there are few, if any, misunderstandings, grievances, errors, personality conflicts, emotional upsets and so on. . . . Getting your message across is the essence of good personal relations.

—Ted Pollack

Resource C

References

Adams, J. Donald. (1963). *The magic & mystery of words.* New York: Holt, Rinehart & Winston. 114 pp. (A classic in the field by a former editor of the *New York Times Book Review.)*

Axtell, Robert E. (1991). *Gestures.* New York: John Wiley. 221 pp. (Do's and don'ts of body language around the world.)

Bly, B. (Ed.). (1999). *Bits and pieces for salespeople: Wit and wisdom to inspire your sales success.* Fairfield, NJ: The Economics Press.

Boothman, Nicholas. (2000). *How to make people like you in 90 seconds or less.* New York: Workman.

Brewer, Ernest W. (1997). *13 proven ways to get your message across.* Thousand Oaks, CA: Corwin Press. (An essential reference for teachers, trainers, presenters, and speakers.)

Capaldi, Nicholas. (1987). *How to win every argument.* New York: MJF Books. 213 pp. (A classic guide to critical thinking.)

Coleman, Paul. (2000). *How to say it to your kids.* Upper Saddle River, NJ: Prentice Hall. 251 pp. (A parents-only communication guide.)

Faber, Adele, & Mazlish, Elaine. (1980). *How to talk so kids will listen and listen so kids will talk.* New York: Avon Books. 233 pp. (A parents' skill book.)

Griffin, Jack. (1994). *How to say it best.* Upper Saddle River, NJ: Prentice Hall. 331 pp. (Choice words, phrases, and model speeches for every occasion.)

Herman, Jeff. (2001). *Insider's guide to book editors, publishers & literary agents.* Rocklin, CA: Prima.

Hitchner, Kenneth W., Tifft-Hitchner, Anne, & Apostol, E. Andre. (1991). *School counselor's letter book.* West Nyack, NY: Center for

Applied Research in Education. 265 pp. (Letter, memos, policy statements, information sheets, and more for every aspect of school counseling in Grades K–12.)

Holm, Kirsten. (Ed.). (various years). *Writer's market*. Cincinnati, OH: Writer's Digest Books.

Kelly, Lynn. (2000). *Don't ask for the dead man's golf clubs*. New York: Workman.

King, Larry. (1994). *How to talk to anyone, anytime, anywhere*. New York: Three Rivers Press. 220 pp. (Secrets of good communication.)

Kosmoski, Georgia J., & Pollack, Dennis R. (2000). *Managing difficult, frustrating, and hostile conversations*. Thousand Oaks, CA: Corwin Press. 103 pp. (Strategies for savvy administrators.)

Kosmoski, Georgia J., & Pollack, Dennis R. (2001). *Managing conversations with hostile adults*. Thousand Oaks, CA: Corwin Press. 111 pp. (Strategies for teachers.)

Maggio, Rosalie. (1990). *How to say it*. Upper Saddle River, NJ: Prentice Hall. 423 pp. (Choice words, phrases, sentences, and paragraphs for every occasion.)

Mamchak, R. Susan, & Mamchak, Steven R. (1990). *The new encyclopedia of school letters*. Upper Saddle River, NJ: Prentice Hall. 397 pp. (Model letters, memos, forms, and bulletins.)

McEwan, Elaine K. (1998). *How to deal with parents who are angry, troubled, afraid or just plain crazy*. Thousand Oaks, CA: Corwin Press. 89 pp. (Strategies for dealing with parents who are out of control.)

Purky, William. (2000). *What students say to themselves*. Thousand Oaks, CA: Corwin Press. 103 pp. (What students say to themselves about themselves.)

Ramsey, Robert D. (2006). *Lead, follow, or get out of the way: How to be a more effective leader in today's schools*. Thousand Oaks, CA: Corwin Press.

Ramsey, Robert D. (2007). *Inspirational quotes, notes, and anecdotes that honor teachers and teaching*. Thousand Oaks, CA: Corwin Press. 131 pp. (Tributes to the greatest profession.)

Spence, Gerry. (1996). *How to argue and win every time*. Griffin, NY: St. Martin's. 292 pp. (Winning arguments at home, at work, in court, everywhere, every day.)

Swets, Paul. (1983). *The art of talking so that people will listen*. New York: Simon & Schuster. 179 pp. (A guide to getting through to family, friends, and business associates.)

Index

The Corwin Press logo—a raven striding across an open book—represents the union of courage and learning. Corwin Press is committed to improving education for all learners by publishing books and other professional development resources for those serving the field of PreK–12 education. By providing practical, hands-on materials, Corwin Press continues to carry out the promise of its motto: **"Helping Educators Do Their Work Better."**